The Presence

The Story of "Smitty"

Missionary to the Philippines

Ron Smith

The Presence

By Ron Smith

ALL RIGHTS RESERVED

No portion of this publication may be reproduced, stored in any electronic system or transmitted in any form or by any means, electronic, mechanical, photocopy, recording or otherwise, without the written permissions from the author and publisher. Brief quotations may be used in literary reviews.

Scripture quotations taken from the New American Standard Bible® (NASB),
Copyright © 1960, 1962, 1963, 1968, 1971, 1972, 1973, 1975, 1977, 1995 by The Lockman Foundation
Used by permission. www.Lockman.org
Unless otherwise noted, all scripture references are taken from the New American Standard Version of the Holy Bible

Copyright © 2017 Ron Smith

All rights reserved.

ISBN-13: 978-1539385714

ISBN-10: 153938571X

Forward

Even though I go to sleep at night around 9 or 10pm, I was consistently waking up at about 1am in the morning and could not go back to sleep for at least 3 hours. So for years now, that has been my sleeping pattern. The middle of the night is a time that I have just come to accept as "being wide awake time". Now I look forward to it, but at first, I laid in bed for hours fighting to try and go back to sleep. When I realized that that wasn't going to happen, I started getting out of bed and watching TV until I got hungry, had a little snack and then when my eyes became heavy again about 4am, drift off for a few more hours.

In June of 2015, after a powerful encounter with God, I finally started using this time in the middle of the night for something more productive, which was writing. I had several people up to that time tell me that I should write a book about my life story and each time I was told that, it witnessed true in my spirit. I knew that that was something I was going to have to do if I wanted to fulfill my purpose and continue to walk forward into the assignment and destiny that the Almighty has for me.

So, most of what you are about to read was typed into my desktop computer at about 2 or 3 in the morning. The Holy Spirit took me back through each individual event in detail that I have written about in this book. Out of all the things that I wrote, edited and re-wrote about, the squatter area of "Pineda" is what would continuously wreck me the most. Even now as I write this forward, I want to bust out again in tears just thinking about the precious adults and children that lived beside the polluted Pasig river in Manila. We should never doubt the Creators heart for his creation.

Ron

Acknowledgements

First and foremost, my family which consists of my Filipina wife, Juliet who goes by the nickname "Merlie" and our three children, Robbie 23, Jasmine 20 and Jacob (the tallest) age 16. I love you with all my heart and thank you for putting up with me when I have displayed the imperfections of humanity. I believe we are on an upward swing and we will all finish strong.

To my older brother Rick for giving me consent to use his life in this story. All he asked was that if it is not true, don't print it. I am so proud of you and how you have turned your life around. I am also glad you were not successful in your plan to end it all early.

Next, Pastor Richard Probasco, who I had the delight of sitting under in my early formative years at New Song Church in Portland, Oregon. Your obedience to God's directives in your life provided shelter and covering for myself and many others as God has used you mightily.

To the Gideons International, founded in 1899 and the oldest association of Christian Professional Businessmen in the USA. Along with their wives, this is the group of men that places Bibles in motel rooms and freely hands them out to prisoners, police, fire and military personnel and to students (5th grade and above) on their campuses.

Lastly, Dr. Myles Munroe, although you have graduated to Heaven at an early age, your teachings on the "Kingdom of God", "Vision" and "Releasing Your Potential" have made an enormous impact on my life and is one of the main reasons I was able to bring this project to completion. I am in your debt sir.

Table of Contents

FORWARD V

ACKNOWLEDGEMENTS VII

TABLE OF CONTENTS IX

THE PRESENCE 1

LOOK UP RON 15

LIGHTS FROM HEAVEN 34

THE TENNIS CENTER 46

THE CALL WAS STILL THERE 57

IN THE MAN'S OFFICE! 67

ARE THOSE CLOUDS? 81

RON THE EVANGELIST 94

WHAT IS VISION? 109

WHERE IS THE WEALTHIEST PLACE ON THE PLANET? 121

ABOUT THE AUTHOR 128

The Presence

It's about time I wrote this. I have so much to share. I feel like I have enough material to fill several books! This is a story about a life that was protected by the Almighty, although most of the time not realized.

I have to start back in high school at the small town in NE Oregon that I grew up in, "Elgin". Elgin boasted a population of about 1,600 with the economic center being the Boise Cascade Wood Mill in town. I have to say that back then, that God was one of the furthest things from my mind and daily thinking.

My family and I were not believers or involved in any church. Actually, there was a church right across the street from my parent's house that I used to stand and look out the living room window at. Sometimes when the people were going in and out I would say to myself, "What a bunch of weak minded people, needing the crutch of church to get through and handle life." Of course, I thought I had it all together and that I had the world by the tail. I know now that that was only the power of pride blinding me in my ignorance.

I had three amazing encounters with the Spirit of God when I was in high school. These all happened in my last year as a senior. One day as I was walking down the hallway at school, I suddenly felt this "Presence" all around me.

The experience was strong and it felt like "something" or "someone" was visiting me right there in broad daylight. I had never experienced anything like it before. It was very unusual because accompanied with this "someone" or "something" visiting me, came this overwhelming desire to go somewhere.

I suddenly wanted to go to the Philippines with every fiber of my being. The experience was very strange because I had no idea why I wanted to go there. I don't think I even knew where the Philippine Islands were on a map or a globe, nor did I know there were over 7,100 islands that made up the Philippines.

They heard the sound of the LORD God walking in the garden in the cool of the day, and the man and his wife hid themselves from the presence of the LORD God among the trees of the garden. Genesis 3:8

I didn't think much about it as the experience was brief and I quickly dismissed it and went on with my day. This same scenario would happen two more times in the hallway that school year and grew stronger each time. The third time the "visitation" happened, I stopped in the hallway, I looked left, then right and then I looked up and said, "Where is this coming from?" Honestly, it was very frustrating. Why did I feel like "someone" or "something" was visiting me and why did I suddenly, overwhelmingly want to go to the Philippines? Of all places on the planet, why the Philippines?

Well, little did I know that God was knocking! All three encounters were brief and I quickly dismissed each experience and quickly went back to what I thought was important, which was trying to hang out with the right guys, because they attracted the right girls and where was I going to go and party Friday night!

Even though I was not consciously asking for the reason and purpose for my existence, I believe that I was silently, subconsciously crying out for validation. I would not be able to connect the Philippines and the "Presence" experience for another 3 years, just before I turned 21. I did not know what I wanted to do with my life. I had no direction or something special that intrigued me or caught my interest (other than the above mentioned girls and partying, which I was confident held a great future).

I was a pretty good athlete. A born natural at just about any sport I tried. I loved to play baseball and I stood out in little league and in high school making county all star teams that traveled to tournaments. I finally played football my senior year only because some of the guys kept hounding me every year with, "Are you going to play football this year Smith?" Of course, I had to prove my manhood, so I played my senior year.

My junior year in basketball, two varsity players were kicked off of the team because they were caught drinking beer at a party. A friend and I were moved up from the junior varsity team to fill the vacant spots on the bench for varsity games. Wouldn't you know it, lightning struck and the basketball team that year went on to take first place at the state tournament. I had a great seat for the championship games and even got in once because we were 20 points up. Oh, and I can't forget, I was introduced by my JR High PE teacher to tennis which I played in the summer. I actually took first place in one of our local tournaments when I was in high school.

My Leader

I had a friend (who we thought should remain anonymous) in high school who I considered my fearless leader. He was the one from whom I first remember being nicknamed, "Smitty".

He was also the best I had ever seen and witnessed when it came to girls and partying. Whatever my friend wanted to do, we did and wherever he wanted to go, we went! Well, my friend went to college after high school so, so did I! If he would have gone into the military, I would have been a Marine or a Navy man. Our first year after high school, my friend and I moved 73 miles away from hometown Elgin to Pendleton, Oregon (population 14,000) and started attending Blue Mountain Community College.

It was general studies for me with a course in scuba diving, last man on the tennis team and at age 18, as much beer drinking as humanly possible.

My friend was amazing and very creative! He put on a three piece suit and drove my 1970 Plymouth Barracuda (wish I would have kept it because I was told recently it could be worth up to $100,000 now) with a 383 pistol grip four speed down to an interview with the owners of a house we wanted to rent.

I need to tell you why we were looking for a house to rent. It's because we were getting kicked out of the apartment we first moved into. (Living on the second floor right above the manager of the apartment complex was not working.) Anyway, my friend convinced these incredibly wonderful older folks that he was on his lunch hour from the bank that he worked at in town. They believed him and they got exactly what they did not want, college kids in their rental.

We discovered how to buy kegs of beer for our parties and soon we were on the Pendleton police's radar. It helped of course that one of our friends was a senior that year and the star running back on the football team for Pendleton High School. All the kids that partied were at our house when we had our "gatherings"! I had never seen so many pretty girls and they were all in my house!

Youth helped us survive that first year in college; I hate to think how fast a lifestyle like that now would almost instantly kill me. When you open your doors like that, many things begin to arrive; marijuana was one of those things. Kids needed a place to smoke pot and experiment and our door was open most of the time. I still remember trying to convince my parents that marijuana was that days "modern day martini." That started an almost three year run of being a cloud of smoke just about everywhere I went.

Year two of college saw my friend and I heading down to Ashland, Oregon, because he wanted to play football. We had also read somewhere in a magazine that the college in Ashland, "Southern Oregon University" was the place to be because it was ranked nationally as a "Party School" and we were all about that!

We were still considered freshman, so we had no choice but to live in the dorms. Greensprings "C" was to be my temporary home for the next few months. I say months because it did not take us long to get kicked out of the dorms, which got us kicked out of school!

My friend did play a little football and I was able to work out with the tennis team for awhile. That is where I met "Keith" the son of a doctor from Bakersfield, California, who grew up with a tennis court in his backyard. Keith was the best player I had ever seen and would be part of the reason I headed to Southern California a year or so later in search of my destiny. I will share with you more on the California trip and Keith later.

It was time to re-group after being expelled from Southern Oregon University. This is where my anonymous friend and I went our separate ways. He eventually ended up on the campus at University of Oregon in Eugene where he graduated with a degree in business and has gone on to a very successful career.

Home was the only option I could think of so, back to Elgin I headed to Mom and Dad's. I had no idea what I wanted to do until I read in a tennis magazine about a five day tennis clinic in San Francisco. This clinic was put on by a recognized international tennis instructor by the name of Dennis Van Der Meer. Dennis owned a big facility on the East coast and was in San Francisco for the clinic. I thought to myself, "I am only young once and if I am ever going to make it on the professional circuit as a player, I had better get to that clinic."

Besides, sitting on the floor for a month at Mom and Dad's watching TV and eating peanut butter and jelly sandwiches was getting old. The clinic was where I met "Bob." More on Bob later and how destiny used him to get me to the Portland area.

I mailed off $500 for the clinic, loaded up my mid-sixties Mazda station wagon/motorhome and tooled off into the sunset. The Mazda was my motorhome because with the back seat folded flat and a foam pad rolled out, it made a pretty good sleeper! My medium sized cooler worked as a fridge, keeping my mayonnaise and lunch meat cool and from spoiling. I said goodbye to my parents and told them I did not know when I would be back.

My plan was to hit up the tennis clinic in San Francisco and then head south to Bakersfield for endless days and nights of playing tennis with "Keith." (Who had moved back home after a short stay at Southern Oregon University) My goal was to see just how good I could get at the game. I planned to use the clinic as my launching pad to international stardom. I knew I was going to learn valuable strategies, work out and drill, drill, drill.

Well, I arrived at the clinic only to be greatly disappointed. I found out when I arrived that I didn't even know what I had spent the $500 on. This was a clinic to learn how to become a certified tennis teacher/instructor. Dennis began to instruct us how to teach the sport. What! I was there to workout, drill, learn new strategies, get in shape and fulfill my destiny as a professional player!

I decided to stay for the duration of the 5 day clinic because they wouldn't give me my money back. Anyway, the clinic is where I met "Bob". Bob was headed back up to Portland, Oregon after the clinic and had planned to open an indoor facility to teach tennis. He invited me to join him in Portland after the clinic. I appreciated the invite but I knew the international tennis circuit was still my destiny and besides, Keith was waiting for me in Bakersfield.

I drove south and caught up with Keith after the clinic eager to start playing tennis full-time. Something had changed and Keith did not seem too interested anymore in my friendship and helping me get to the top of the International circuit. Unfortunately, we parted our ways and I was left with a life altering decision of "What was I going to do now?" My whole goal was to get to Southern California and fulfill my destiny.

Looking at a map that I carried in my motorhome, I detected a city to the East that held intrigue; Las Vegas Baby! Home of an international tennis star named "Andre Agassi" and the UNLV "Rebels" College and Division 1 tennis team. Something Andre Agassi and I had in common, being a rebel. I still remembered the tennis world being on edge and in shock as Andre surprised everyone during his second or third appearance at Wimbledon and finally wore traditional white tennis clothing for the tournament in jolly old England! Ah, those were the days! A non-violent Rebel! (You probably have to be at least 40 years old to remember the camera named after him)

I made it to Vegas and quickly located the campus and the outdoor tennis courts and to my surprise was in the midst of one of the largest groups of aspiring players that I had ever seen. I introduced myself to a few of them and quickly landed an invitation to "work out" with the junior varsity team.

I really wasn't interested in going to school, I just wanted to play! I think I showed up for a few days in a row before reality started to set in. When I left Oregon for my world tour, I had a certain amount of money and I knew almost to the dollar what I needed for gas to get back home if things did not work out. I was getting to the "almost out" portion of my money and I knew if I was going to stay much longer I was going to have to secure employment. So, pulling on my 3 years of job experience in high school, I went to a grocery store and picked up an application.

I don't think I ever filled out the application or took it back to the store and a few days later as I was laying on my back in the motorhome and reflecting, I realized I had no choice; it was time to head back to the living room rug at Mom and Dad's in Elgin.

Thank God I was pretty accurate as to the amount of gas money I needed for the trip. I made it all the way back to La Grande (which was 20 miles from home) and I was on nothing but fumes in the gas tank. I had no choice but to pull into a gas station and ask the young fellow who came out to help me if he was interested in a few of my choicest 8 track tapes for two dollars of gas (yes, 8 track tapes) so I could get home. It was already late at night and luckily, he was a music fan of some of my finest.

I can still vividly remember my Dad's face and tone of voice the next morning when he laid eyes on me after my 3 to 4 week absence. He said something like, "Well look, the world traveler is home." He didn't seem too excited to see me. I can't blame him, I had had no contact with my parents the whole time I was gone and they had had little or no idea where I was or what I was doing. Part of the rebel in me I guess. Anyway, it was time to regroup again and my parents graciously let me stay.

My Dad was a supervisor at the Boise Cascade wood mill in town and seemed successful at just about any time he thought I needed a job. I had worked at the mill the summer after high school before Blue Mt Community College and then again the summer before my second "attempt" at college in Ashland at Southern Oregon University. I could probably get back on at the mill but it wasn't exactly what I wanted to do. I saw something in high school that sort of scared me; guys graduating from Elgin High, getting married and then going to work at the mill for the rest of their lives. I was determined to see the world and did not want to fall "into step" with my Elgin brethren.

In a vacuum of no direction, common sense and my Dad won over as I found myself working graveyard at the mill. I remember standing out on the metal "catwalk" with a 16ft aluminum pike pole in my hands that we used to push the floating logs under us onto the ramp that took them up to be peeled. I had a sensation one day as the sun was coming up and daylight was upon us that, "You know what, I have seen the world" and a strange sense came over me that being at the mill for the rest of my life seemed OK and actually comforting.

There I was, a chew of tobacco in my lip, leather gloves on my hands, in command of a pike pole and thinking this was going to be alright! Was it time to settle down? Nonsense! Destiny shook me again out of my slumber just a few weeks later and I knew I had to get out of town.

It has been said that, and is worth repeating,

"The greatest enemy to fulfilling your purpose and God given potential is being satisfied with your last success."

Putting your feet up and relishing in your accomplishments can be dangerous to you fulfilling your potential and reaching your goals! I had seen a "part" of the world and something was trying to get me to be satisfied with this. After all, I did go to Vegas!

"Unfulfillment" settled in again and I began to search my data bank for anything I could grab onto that would give me my next direction. I was definitely in search of something. Making the professional circuit as a tennis player was suddenly not all that appealing, but I still had a sense of destiny and I felt compelled to push on into the unseen, the unknown.

I had actually had several experiences up to this point in my life that I would have difficulty explaining if asked to. Several times I had had this sensation that there was a higher, deeper purpose for my life, that there was another reason why I was born, another reason for my existence other than what I was currently experiencing.

I had this sense that I was not a biological accident or a mistake. The frustrating thing was, is that I did not know what that higher purpose or reason for my existence was. This is what, in part, propelled me forward to making, some would say "risky decisions" and not falling into step with the flow of my fellow high school graduates around me. Besides, up until now, I would have considered myself very unlucky when it came to "Love" and I had no serious prospects waiting around that would be happy with living in Elgin for the rest of their lives, even though that would have been a good life.

Time for Bob

It was time for Bob! I must have saved his phone number from our encounter at the clinic in San Francisco because I found myself a few weeks later heading to Portland, Oregon in my motorhome. Bob welcomed me with open arms and invited me to stay with him and his girlfriend in Lake Oswego, a Portland suburb. I think his girlfriend owned the big expensive home where he lived.

I soon found out that Bob had rented an old "National Guard" armory building and had painted a tennis surface on the floor and put up a tennis net. The ceiling was not really high enough for competitive play, but it made a very good place to teach lessons. I soon found out that Bob had a "side business" and was probably making more money selling marijuana then he was teaching tennis lessons.

I will never forget one morning at the house when Bob came out of his bedroom in a panicked hurry to get to "work" and he said, "Now where did I put that joint?" I thought it very odd that I had to point out the fact that it was hanging out of his mouth. Anyway, that was kind hearted Bob, a licensed professional to teach tennis.

Somehow the tennis coach for Mt Hood Community College from nearby Gresham, Oregon, (another suburb of Portland) showed up at our tennis facility one day. I think he brought a student to give a lesson to. Anyway, we ended up knocking the ball around a little bit which ended up in an invitation for me to receive a financial scholarship if I would come out for the team at the college. I was elated about the opportunity and soon found myself a full-time student.

So, it was back to school and working out with a tennis team. My younger brother "Russ" had just graduated from Elgin High School and was offered a scholarship to run cross country and track at the same college as well. When he showed up on campus, I found myself beginning to run with his team to get in shape for tennis. I really don't know how I did all this because I was continuing to mistreat my body with drugs and alcohol. I spent 5 semesters going to Mt Hood CC and still never finished my two year degree.

I was starting to reach a breaking point in my life. I was beginning to get tired of my partying lifestyle. It has been said that "sin is pleasurable for a season", and I was beginning to realize that all this so called "fun" and "pleasure" was not helping me get to where I wanted to go in life. Just a few years back, I thought I had discovered what I wanted to do with my life, which was party and stay high. That was working for awhile; now, not so much. I was beginning to see that the friends I was associating with were living only for their next party or to get high.

I was also beginning to figure out that after three years of this lifestyle that it was beginning to slowly kill me. I started to notice that the friends I was spending a lot of time with were quickly headed down a dead end street. I also realized that if I kept up this lifestyle and these "friends", that I was going to continue down that street with them. This began to deeply concern me because I envied my father, who was young at heart, enjoying life and growing old in Elgin. I wanted to grow old and enjoy life like my Dad and I saw that in order to accomplish this that I was going to have to change directions. I decided that I would put a stop to this downward death spiral I suddenly found myself in. I was out of control and I was going to change that. I decided that I was going to quit, that I was going to "turn over a new leaf" and start to live a clean and sober life. Growing old and enjoying life here I come!

Well, I tried and I tried and I tried. I broke smoking devices or "bongs" and flushed marijuana down the toilet. I would attempt to break free and stay clean for a few days maybe even a week, but would fall right back into the death cycle with gusto because I hadn't been high for almost a week! It was very frustrating and a terribly depressing cycle. It did not take me long to figure out that I was trapped and that I was not going to be able to break free. I quickly began to give up hope of ever breaking free and living a full, long and productive life. My "pleasurable fun" had turned into a "freaking" nightmare.

I'm Trapped!

The only thing I could see in my immediate future was never being free from these substances and that I would probably die a horrible drug induced death at a young age because the experimentation with substances had already gotten way past just marijuana. I could tell if I wasn't able to stop now that it was only going to get worse.

I was beginning to accept my mortality; for up to this point, for some reason, I thought I was going to live forever. Suddenly, life became so futile, so meaningless. I told myself that even if I did break free and live a long productive life, you know; make a million dollars, marry and have a happy family, have homes around the world; what's the use or the purpose? In the end you just die anyway and probably don't remember any of the good life you had had because, well, you're just dead.

Then I began to reason that what is the sense of sticking around for another 10 or 20 years and then die, why not just get it over with now and save myself the years of torture? I considered myself a reasonably intelligent person, so I asked myself, "Why stick around, beat my head against a brick wall and then die, why not do myself a favor and quicken the process along?" As you can see, I needed some answers. I didn't know I was searching for Jesus the anointed King, but suddenly, all I wanted to know was the answer to this question,

"Is there life after death?"

Because either way I looked at it, whether I broke free into a clean, sober and successful life or not, "death" was inevitable and up to this point, I hadn't run into anyone that had any answers as how to get past it. I know now that Jesus said, "I am the Truth, the Life and the Way and if you search for Him with all your heart, guaranteed, you will find Him"! The question, "Why not get it over with early" at this point in my life, seemed reasonable and one that there most certainly should be an answer for. As I seriously considered suicide, I became very curious about what I was going to find or where I was going to find myself if I followed through with this newly considered "pain, frustration and addiction relief" solution. I didn't understand what was happening at the time, but God quickly began to direct my thoughts and my attention to the night sky.

Almost like being forced, I began to remember back to my days in JR High School (age 12 & 13) when I would sleep out in the backyard of my parents home in the summer time with my neighborhood buddies. One thing we loved to do in the middle of the night was to climb on top of the grade school and other commercial buildings that were downtown Elgin. I have to share one experience I had with my buddy named "Momo".

We were running around on top of the grade school one night, when we noticed the police circling the block in their patrol car and shining a search light toward the roof. We had been discovered and someone had obviously turned us in. Adrenaline running extremely high, we climbed off the front side of the building in an effort to escape capture. Once on the ground, we ran (like idiots) around the corner of the building, not knowing that just 30 yards down this side of the building was one of the officers standing on the sidewalk with flashlight in hand and scanning the roof. There was another officer in the car beside him and when we ran around in plain view, they both saw us. In shock, Momo and I turned around and ran back from the direction we had come. I remember the officer's equipment hanging from his belt that began "jingling" and the car engine racing as the chase was on. As soon as we got back around the corner and out of sight, it dawned on me that Momo was faster than me and I was surely going to jail. So, I dove behind the tall bushes that were beside the building and laid motionless on the ground. I then watched the officers run and drive right past me chasing my friend. Anyway, they never caught us as Momo outran them. I lack the space to share more adventures.

Back to my parents backyard, I remember laying on my back at night in my sleeping bag with my hands tucked behind my head for long periods of time just gazing at the stars and the great expanse of space! At almost 21 years old, the memories of my JR High experiences as a young man in my parent's backyard at night came flooding back to me absolutely unstoppable.

Look Up Ron

I literally felt like I was being bombarded by these memories of gazing at the stars and the expanse and beauty of the night sky. Having this come back to me so aggressively and forcefully caused me to take a life changing interest in the expanse of creation all around me. I started to look up and ask myself, "Does the universe ever stop? Is there an end to it when you look straight up?" I quickly came to the conclusion that it does not stop, in fact it goes on forever and ever. My mind tried to convince me that at the end of the universe was a brick wall with a sign on it that said, "End of the Universe" and that I should not even bother looking on the other side of the brick wall because there wasn't anything there. I knew right away that that was crazy and I knew if there was a brick wall out there, there had to be something on the other side! It had to go on forever! I started to ask myself for the first time, "Wait a minute, where did all this come from?" This is much bigger than I had ever thought or considered. There were three possibilities or theories that came to me almost immediately and they came in rapid fire.

The first thought I had was to consider Darwin's Theory, you know, the one where we evolved from something that crawled out of the ocean, grew legs and walked upright, turning into monkeys and then into man as we are today. The second possibility was that there was suddenly this great big "Bang" and everything just popped into existence. The third and final possibility that came to me was that there was a supernatural "something" way out there "somewhere" that fashioned all this, a Creator.

I thought extremely long and hard about these options. Something drew me forward and I would not be satisfied until I found the answer for the origin of myself and the universe.

In my search, common sense convinced me that the first two were dismissible, but the thought of a "supernatural something way out there somewhere that created all this" seemed very appealing to me and I started to lean toward it. I began to feel like it "held water" and it did not take very long until I became convinced that there had to be a Creator God!

A Creator! Someone, something, way out there somewhere, had to be the answer! An endless creation demanded an Endless Creator. An incredible design demanded the existence of an Incredible Designer. I quickly realized that all of the wrong things that I thought I had done hidden in darkness and in secret, thinking I was getting away with, that someone, somewhere had been watching me the whole time. Suddenly, the fear of God came upon me and hence; the beginning of wisdom.

The fear of the LORD is the beginning of wisdom; A good understanding have all those who do His commandments; His praise endures forever. Psalms 111:10

I became instantly convinced that there was a Creator and that someone had been watching me my entire life. I thought about this new-found conclusion that common sense brought me to and it did not take me long to move on to the next set of conclusions. I believed that He had to be somewhere out there and that 1) He must be intelligent, 2) He must be powerful and the attribute that struck me the strongest was that 3) He must have the ability to communicate.

It dawned on me also at this time that, "Hey, I have some intelligence, I have some power and I can communicate." My new-found understanding of "There has to be a creator of the universe" and "He has to have the ability to communicate" really started to excite me.

Side note; I like science fiction, futuristic movies and I just want to give a shout out to Jodi Foster for her movie, "Contact". Dear Jodi, I pray that you continue to search for Him, for I know He desires to reveal Himself to you!

Yes, if there is a God and He can make all this creation that I was suddenly becoming aware of, then communication would be easy for Him. Of course He could communicate. I quickly realized and believed that if I cried out to Him, that He would reveal Himself to me and that I could make contact and communicate with Him. I believed that and I started to get really excited about the possibility of not only believing in Him but actually coming to know Him and making contact and having a conversation with Him.

So, I looked up and started to quietly ask, "Who are you, I want to know you?" I felt like I did not have to shout because surely He was not hard of hearing. I expected to hear a booming voice from the sky, something that sounded like, "I AM that I AM!" I consciously asked the question over and over many times that first day, expecting an answer. After a few days, I thought I should have heard from Him by now but had not, so I started asking more aggressive and of course, louder. Within four or five days, out of desperation, I was shouting at the sky. I was beyond just desperate. I really needed Him to respond to my cry for help and validation.

The Gideon

This is the condition I found myself in on the day I entered the open square in the middle of the Mt Hood Community College campus. Desperation must have been written all over my face. There were probably 100 students in this open square that day trying to get to different parts of the campus. I entered the square weaving between students that seemed to be going in all directions. It was the 10 minute break and everybody wanted to get to their next class.

As I walked and tried to miss students, I believe God directed my attention to my left about 10 to 12 yards away where I glanced at a young man standing behind a small table with some little books on it. This young man behind the table was also having a conversation with another young man that was standing in front of the table. I didn't think anything of it and I looked back to make sure I did not run into any oncoming students. I dodged a few more students and being led by God again (although I had no idea what was happening) I looked to my left again, almost over my shoulder, at the young man behind the table. Something happened that was very, very strange. Out of all the people in this open square that the young man behind the table could have been looking at, for some reason, the second time I looked, he was looking right at me.

Instantly, I was embarrassed and shocked at making eye contact like that with a stranger. I put my head down and quickened my pace trying to get away from this uncomfortable situation and put it behind me. Well, I took about 10 more steps and it was with my head still down, after dodging a few more students, when I realized that there was someone directly in front of me that would not let me get around them. I was forced to look up and to my shock again, there was that young man who seconds ago was behind the table.

The first thing I noticed when I looked up was the great big smile on his face and his eyes that locked onto mine. He introduced himself and then stuck out his hand, offering to shake mine. I responded with a handshake and I think I said my name back. Then he asked me a question, "Would you like one of these?" as he held out and offered, no doubt, one of the little books that I had seen a few seconds ago from his table. I looked at the little book and then back at him and I asked, "What is it?" He told me that it was a New Testament, Psalms and Proverbs. I had no idea what that was at all. It was decision time and fortunately, I was thinking quick on my feet that day.

I did not know if I wanted the little book this bold evangelist was offering, but I said to myself, "If I take it, maybe he will let me go" and I would be set free from this strange and incredibly uncomfortable encounter. So, I reached out and took it. He responded by saying, "Great, have a nice day" and then he turned and walked away, probably going back to his table. My plan had worked! He was gone and I was free! I put the little book in my pocket and went on to class relieved that that was over.

When I got home later that day, out of curiosity, I took out the little green book and started thumbing through the pages. I had no idea what I had in my hands. I was still asking the Creator to reveal Himself. I wanted to know Him, I wanted to communicate, not just believe in Him and of course I still wanted to know if there was life after death.

As I looked through the book, I noticed right away the guide to "Feelings" and "Answers to some of Life's Problems" in the first few pages. Three of them spoke to me very clearly and defined my situation almost perfectly. The first was, "Are you lonely?" Are you kidding me? I was so lonely; I thought I was going to die. Second, "Friends Fail?" Are you kidding me again? I felt like I had not one true friend. Not one! I had had plenty of "fair weather friends" you know the type, when you have a car, gas and beer in plenty, you have friends. But where were these friends when the mess had to be cleaned up the next morning and your car needed gas? Third, "Need Guidance?" Yes! Hello! I am considering ending my life early, a little guidance and direction at this point would be very good.

Needless to say, those three topics resonated with me very, very strongly. I turned to the directed pages and passages and started to read what I still did not know was the Bible for the very first time. I would find out later that the young man that ran me down (he had to of run) on that college campus and gave me the little book was part of the "Gideon Bible Society."

The Gideon Bible Society is an international, voluntary organization that prints and distributes Bibles. They freely place them in motels, hand them out on military bases, to police forces and to students in public places like high schools and college campuses. (There will be more on the Gideons later because I became a volunteer Gideon myself.)

As I began to read, almost immediately something powerful began to happen. I found myself mysteriously drawn to this little book. Something was stirring on the inside of me and there was a hunger that was quickly growing. With every fiber of my being, I wanted to spend more time reading it. Actually, I had a hard time putting the little book down. The only other book I could liken it too was JR Tolkien's, "The Hobbit" series that I read in high school. You know what I mean, six hours into it and your eyeballs are beginning to burn but it is so captivating you can't put it down.

To my mind, nothing was making any sense at all, but to my heart, on the inside of me, something was stirring wildly. It was almost like something on the inside of me was dead or had been sleeping and that it was beginning to flip and flop back and forth, waking up, gasping for air and coming alive.

This went on for about three days and one evening I was up really late (around 11pm) sitting up in my bed and reading. Something very exciting was happening although; I had no idea what it was. I could not get enough of this little book, could not put it down and when I finished a page, I could not turn to the next fast enough.

I didn't know I was searching for Jesus, all I knew is that I was searching for the truth to the questions; "Is there life after death?' and "How do I make contact with this Creator?" God promises that if we search for Him with all of our heart, we will find Him!

I was searching for something at the early age of 21 that many people put off or wait to do until they are on their death beds and unfortunately, some not even then. The half hearted "seeker" or "casual inquirer" will not have the same dramatic results that I did. I realize I was being unusual.

And you will seek Me and find Me, when you search for me with all your heart. Jeremiah 29:13

I am the way, the truth and the life; no one comes to the Father but through me. John 14:6

Ask, and it will be given to you; seek, and you will find; knock, and it will be opened to you. For everyone who asks receives, and he who seeks finds, and to him who knocks, it will be opened. Matthew 7:7-8

And the testimony is this, that God has given us eternal life, and this life is in His Son. He who has the Son has the life; he who does not have the Son of God does not have the life. These things I have written to you who believe in the name of the Son of God, in order that you may know that you have eternal life. 1 John 5:11-13

I wish that I could remember the exact verse that I was reading in the book of "John" at approximately 11 o'clock that night when all of a sudden, the words jumped off of the page and God spoke to me very intimately and powerfully. I could also use this term; God's Word was "quickened" to me." The first thing I saw was the availability of "eternal life" or life after the grave and then God said, "My name is Jesus and this eternal life that I just showed you is available through me"!

I really can't explain this experience with justice because I am limited to having to use words. Life eternal opened up right in front of me and I saw it. I saw it! It was like walking up to a cliff and hanging my toes over the edge, looking down and not being able to see the bottom. It went on forever.

God supernaturally showed me life everlasting and that it was available to me. This was one of the answers that I was looking for and I know a really good deal when I see one! I wanted it. I saw that it was available and I wanted the eternal life that this Jesus was offering. A few minutes later I had to ask, "Well, how do I get it?" Nothing else was said or made clear to me at this point, so I started to thumb through the back of the book where I came across this that was written;

"Do you want to receive Jesus Christ as your Lord and Savior? Then say this prayer!"

I thought to myself, "Well, if that's all I have to do to get eternal life, that sounds easy, I can do that." So I read and repeated what was called the "sinner's prayer" out loud saying, "Lord Jesus I confess that I am a sinner, (although I had no idea what a sinner was) please forgive me, come into my life and take control in Jesus name, Amen." To be honest with you, the only thing I understood about that prayer was that I knew I was out of control and I needed someone bigger, more powerful than myself to help.

So, I said the prayer, looked up and checked for any indications, signs or feelings that I had said it correctly and that the Creator had heard me. Nothing was different and it didn't seem that anything had changed. I thought surely if I had said and done it correctly that I would have at least felt something, seen something! I mean, come on! I was left only with my thoughts and doubts of, "Maybe I didn't say it right, I'll try it again."

Well, the doubts that I had not done it correctly and that I did not have it yet (eternal life) only got louder. So, I repeated the prayer again and again hoping for different results. Desperation was already and currently a major part of my life and the fact that I had just been shown the availability of eternal life, followed all the instructions that I had been given up to this point, but still did not know if I was successful in obtaining it, took me to a new level of frustration and desperation that I had never before experienced.

I didn't know if I had to be on my knees when I said the prayer or do I have to be crying when I said the prayer, what was the formula so that I knew, that God knew, I was serious. I wanted to feel something, hear something so that I knew He had heard me because up to this point, I wasn't sure He had. If I had really received eternal life and I really had it, something was surely going to be noticeably different in my life and I wanted to know that now.

He Touched Me

God does not disappoint. He knows what each individual needs and He is faithful. I believe it was the third day after repeating the prayer the first time and asking Jesus to come in and take control of my life, when I had reached a breaking point. I was as close to having an emotional breakdown as I had ever been before. This was unchartered waters. That night, on the third day, desperate to feel something, see something or hear Him assure me, I remember walking into my bedroom completely distraught. My knees hit the floor and my elbows planted on the bed. Then I buried my face in my hands and from somewhere inside me that I had never been before, deep, deep down, (I can't explain it because I have to use words) I cried out to God with all my heart and with great emotion saying, "Father in Heaven…….. Almighty……… God……..!"

What happened next is something that I have never and will never forget. I felt this powerful presence descend on me, it was God the Holy Spirit coming in raw power. It felt like I was being touched with "under control" 220 electricity. His presence was brief and direct. He descended and then just a few seconds later, ascended back from the exact direction He came from, having touched me on my back just below the neckline between my shoulder blades. If the song "He touched me" had not already been written, I surely would have become the author!

The Bible says that the fear of the Lord is the beginning of wisdom. Did that frighten me? You bet it did! When Almighty God in His Spirit form reaches down and touches you with the tip of His little finger, you know you have been contacted and that you have heard from God.

My search was satisfied, temporarily. I had made contact with the Creator or maybe I should say that the Creator made contact with me. As His presence of raw power left the room, it left me almost paralyzed at what I had just experienced for a few brief seconds. I slowly slid up into bed, laid on my right side and pulled the covers up under my chin. Wow, that was powerful! I stopped wondering and crying out for a sign. I could not have handled any more signs and wonders that night. This was the first of three powerful encounters that I had in the first 6 months of my new found relationship with the Creator and with His spiritual realm.

From the night that I first repeated the prayer out of the back of that Gideon New Testament, my life was changed. I just didn't know that I had meant it from my heart the first time and that He had heard me. There had been no one there to teach me that when you receive Christ (and eternal life) as your Lord and Savior, you receive Him and eternal life by "faith" and sometimes faith doesn't trigger any feelings or cause lights to suddenly appear and flash.

The following verse is one of the most important ones that I have ever committed to memory. I simply needed to know!

God has given us eternal life, and this life is in his Son. Whoever has the Son has life; whoever does not have the Son of God does not have life. I write these things to you who believe in the name of the Son of God so that you may know that you have eternal life. 1 John 5:11

By God's design, I had neighbors in my apartment complex that had been inviting me to their church. I'm sure I startled them one day soon after my experience when I told them that I wanted to go! Wow, suddenly I was experiencing a brand new life, relationship, freedom, direction and purpose.

I quickly realized that it had been God speaking to me three years ago in Elgin in my high school hallway when He touched me with His presence. I knew now that the Creator had a plan and that I was to go around the world (the Philippines being central in this direction) and tell people about this Jesus and preach His Kingdom. Wow! Talk about exciting! I remember attending the local church which my neighbors had led me to and from the get-go, felt drawn to walk forward during invitation time in the services.

I think it was during the third or fourth week that I finally overcame the fear of man, stepped out and walked up the aisle in front of the whole church. That was a huge, bold step for me. I believe I was already committed, already saved from my sin, but God was wanting me to show some spine and make it public! So, I went up, talked to the Pastor and said the "sinner's prayer" again with him. Then he asked me if I wanted to be baptized. I had no idea what that really meant but I was very open to whatever He would have said, so that morning right after the service, they dunked me in a tank of water, briefly immersing me completely!

A few years later I would get baptized again at New Song Church in Portland (much, much more on New Song later!) with a little bit more understanding that baptism is a public declaration of a personal and private commitment to God and identifying with the death, burial and resurrection of Christ.

Well, I was off and running with a new direction and connection with Almighty God, ready at any moment to jet around the world and to start proclaiming (to officially announce) the good news of the availability of eternal life in Jesus and that the Kingdom of God was here! Little did I know that it would be almost eight years before I would finally get on that airplane. There was much that had to happen, and many things that had to change in my life.

Singing In the Produce Room

At the time this was happening, along with classes at Mt Hood Community College, I was working part-time for a Fred Myers grocery store in North Portland. I remember being at work one afternoon at the store soon after my experience with His presence in my bedroom and what I will call the "raw power experience." Anyway at the store, the produce department was mine!

I had learned and memorized my first song from church and was singing it loudly in the back room. You know the room separate from the sales floor where you prepare all the fruits and vegetables, then bring them out for display! Anyway, I was belting out the song "Because He Lives" unhindered and with gusto and new found faith. It would be difficult to explain the great excitement, joy and new found energy and freedom I was experiencing. True and pure joy, the God kind of joy, does equal strength! As a matter of fact, The Kingdom of God is not eating and drinking, but righteousness, peace and joy in the Holy Spirit. (Rom 14:17)

Then he said to them, "Go, eat of the fat, drink of the sweet, and send portions to him who has nothing prepared; for this day is holy to our Lord. Do not be grieved, for the joy of the LORD is your strength." Nehemiah 8:10

Some of the words to the song I was singing in the back room go like this:

Because He lives, I can face tomorrow. Because He Lives, all fear is gone. Because I know He holds the future and life is worth the living just because He lives.

One of the aftereffects of making contact with my Creator was a new lease on life. I no longer wanted to end my life early because of hopelessness. Suddenly, I was ready to live, but only, only because He lived and only, only because He and He alone, held the future in His hands! I was discovering my purpose and I was beginning to understand the assignment that God had placed on my life.

Not only did I get my questions answered, "Is there life after death" and "where did all this come from anyway" but I had discovered that I was not a biological accident after all and that I was actually created for and on planet earth for a purpose.

Anyway, back to the produce room! God has blessed me with a very strong voice (notice I did not say sought after quality, just very strong) and I was letting it rip with no care of who might hear me from the back preparation room. I was pretty isolated in that room and wasn't concerned about being overheard. I was working hard at moving 50lb boxes of potatoes around and stacking other boxes of vegetables.....and singing loudly.

Suddenly, I heard voices start to sing with me. Yes, voices! These were voices I heard with my physical ears, not just my heart or inner ear. If you had been in the room with me, I believe you would have heard them also. Well that, to say the least, startled me. Startled me quiet! I stopped singing and froze, then said to myself, "what was that?" The answer came quickly, "Angels Ron, those are Angels singing with you!" "Are you kidding me," I said to myself, "Angels?"

I recovered from my initial shock and quickly started singing again wanting them to join me again in praising our God. They did not disappoint! I never saw them with my physical eyes, but I could tell as I began to sing again that there was a small angelic choir in the room with me. You can tell when you're in a room like that from which direction sound (especially a small choir of angels) is coming from. They were up near the ceiling in one of the corners of the room. I really don't remember how long I sang or how long we sang together again, but it was absolutely amazing. I can't give the experience justice because I am again, limited to using words. One thing is for sure, we are not alone!

I continued going to church and working as a produce man, but going to school was something that suddenly did not make any sense because it just seemed like there wasn't time for such foolishness. I had to save the world, I had to fulfill my destiny as a world evangelist and time was running out! Jesus was coming back soon and I had to tell people about Him!

At the time of the writing of this book, well, that was 35 years ago. I look back on this now, and just maybe, a college education would have been the correct thing to pursue at that time if I would have known what I wanted to study. Although, I believe that sometimes, a college education can get in the way of fulfilling your destiny and the assignment that God has for you. Some people are trapped by their college degree that stops them from operating in their gift!

They spent all this money, effort and time to get an education and can't "throw that away" and serve God in the assignment that He has for them. Sometimes, you have to get away from family and their influences, Abraham had to.

Anyway, I was suddenly this wild eyed evangelist that would talk to anyone, anywhere about Jesus and the eternal life that was available. I was bold, but at times not wise. I was full of zeal for the Lord, but had yet to learn wisdom. I remember going home to Elgin for a visit shortly after this all happened. I just couldn't find the "off" button. If I could corner or trap someone, they were going to hear my story of being touched by the "power" and singing with angels! My parents had to have thought I had gone stark raving mad! I had to apologize to them later because I wouldn't stop until they felt like they had no choice but to leave the room we were in. I basically estranged my entire family from myself. My two brothers, I'm sure, thought I had gone crazy also. None of my family understood me, because I was the first to give my life away to the Savior. I had been radically "saved!"

Therefore, if anyone is in Christ, he is a new creation. The old has passed away; behold, the new has come. 2 Corinthians 5:17

I remember my Mom telling me one day, "We don't know you anymore Ronny!" Wow! I had changed! Now, I don't encourage boldness and zeal for God without tempering it with love and wisdom, but if your own mother says she doesn't know you anymore, then I'd have to say, "You're on the right track!" I recently counseled a new believer to not make the same mistake I made with my family. I told him to just go home and let his changed life speak. You have heard it said, "Preach, evangelize and witness at all opportunities and if necessary, use words." I am sure it would have been different if my family saw the change in me first and had been curious enough to ask what had happened to me.

Of course, I would have sat them down and calmly, lovingly explained the transformation, well, maybe. I will really never know, all I can do now is try to remember wisdom as I go forward from here! And forward, we will go! Thanks for coming along!

Preaching in the Mormon Church

I did something on one of the trips I made back to my hometown of Elgin in that first year as a believer that set me apart with a certain subgroup of "Elginites". After I became a believer, I began learning about the "Latter Day Saints" or "Mormons." I started learning about this religion because I was trying to convert their missionaries. I would see them walking around in their white shirts, ties and name tags, trying to convert people. I would approach them and engage with them in conversation. Sometimes I invited them into my house when they would show up at the door. Anyway, I had a great God given interest in them and they were certainly a challenge. Sometimes, they were the only ones that would entertain this "wild eyed evangelist" that I had become!

I learned that one of our "beloved" high school teachers had been a devout Mormon and that intrigued me and sparked my interest and curiosity to find out who else I had known for years, but never knew that they were a part of the LDS church. I came to the conclusion that for my curiosity to be satisfied, I might just as well visit the local congregation in Elgin, and find out personally for myself.

Believe me, I did not go there to visit because I thought there might be some truth I was missing out on. I went there only to satisfy my curiosity and answer the question, "Who else have I known for years, but did not know they were Mormon?" So, I slipped into the back row of the local LDS church in Elgin one Sunday morning. Just walking in and being there caused quite a stir.

One of the elder gentlemen of their congregation came over, sat next to me and took great interest in who I was and where I was from. He seemed very friendly and I tried to answer all his questions. The service started with about 30 people in attendance. God's timing is incredible! I learned that once a month, there was not a message by one person or preacher, but this was "Testimony Sunday" and I had arrived for it.

I thought it very interesting to see various church members "pop up" from their seats or even walk up to the front and stand behind the pulpit and share an encouraging short story or testimony about, "What the Mormon church had done for them!"

I sat in the back minding my own business when somebody decided that my comfort zone needed a little shook up! Suddenly, God the Holy Spirit was moving mightily inside me and I knew what He was saying and what He wanted me to do. I had felt Him move like this in me before and there was no doubt in my mind.

My gift of evangelism was about to be exercised. My mind started racing, "But what if they get mad and throw me out?" I quickly came to the conclusion that it would be better to die right there than disobey and miss what God had for me. So, I turned to my new found friend that was sitting next to me and asked, "Would it be ok if I shared something?"

He assured me that it would be fine. So, preacher that I am, (or want to be) I grabbed my thick hardbound Dr. Ryrie Study Bible, stood up, walked up the aisle and proceeded to take my place behind the pulpit. Man! It was quiet in that LDS church. I placed my bible on the pulpit with it open to the book of Galatians and proceeded to exhort and encourage the folks there about how family orientated they were. Then I dropped a bomb and said, "But I have a problem with some of your doctrine!" Nobody moved, I wondered if they were even breathing. I looked down and read Galatians chapter 1 verses 6-8.

I am amazed that you are so quickly deserting Him who called you by the grace of Christ, for a different gospel; which is really not another; only there are some who are disturbing you and want to distort the gospel of Christ. But even if we, or an angel from heaven, should preach to you a gospel contrary to what we have preached to you, he is to be accursed! Galatians 1:6-8

Now, some of you might not understand what that meant to most of the precious LDS people there that morning. The "Mormon" church was started by the prophet Joseph Smith about two hundred years ago after a revelation of an angelic visit. Their story goes like this; Joseph was visited by an angel of God called "Moroni" and Moroni gave Joseph golden tablets that contained their "Book of Mormon." Thus, a new revelation that the Bible is the Word of God, but that it is incomplete without the one given by the angel. Now the LDS church was the only church of Christ that held this new revelation and thus was the soul and only possessor of finished and total truth from God. Basically, when I read that, I told them that their church and their theology was off, way off!

When I finished reading that, I looked up and expected a riot to break out. I expected the men in the church to rise up and escort me, no, drag me to the door and throw me in the street! Instead, nobody moved and nobody said anything. You could have heard a pin drop on the carpet in the back of the room!

I knew after staring out over the congregation for about five more seconds, that my assignment there was finished and that I was done. So, I closed my Bible and went and sat back down. I sat there amazed as the service went on as if I had said absolutely nothing. Someone stood up and the stories of "What the Mormon church had done for them," went on as if I had said nothing. Then, my new found friend next to me started to tell me something.

When I looked over at him, I could see that he was very agitated and very upset as he said something like this to me, "I am getting tired of people coming in here and doing that," his countenance had changed drastically. He maintained control of himself and the service soon came to an end. I stood around for a few minutes waiting to see if anyone wanted to talk to me and I noticed, across the room, that several other men were physically detaining my new friend because it was obvious that he wanted a piece of me. I thought that this might be a good time to make my escape, so I headed for the door. Several people greeted me on my way out and then a young girl, probably high school age, came up to me and said, "What was that scripture that you shared?" No doubt, she was one of the main reasons why I was there that morning.

I told her Galatians 1:6-8 and then I left and went home. The Holy Spirit would make a habit of moving on me many times like that again, in different circumstances and countries. I have made it almost a habit to randomly walk into an LDS service from time to time where I live now in La Grande, Oregon just to say "hello." Some of the shocked looks on people's faces that I have known for years here in this community have been priceless.

About six or seven months later, I went home to Elgin again at Christmas time. I heard that the Nazarene Church in town was putting on a special Christmas program called a "Cantata" and I wanted to attend. This event was being held at the "Elgin Opera House" in downtown Elgin, which was not their regular church building. When I got there and discovered that there was an entrance fee, I was disappointed because I didn't bring any money with me. So, I turned around, looked across and down the street and saw that the LDS church was obviously having a Christmas function as well because of all the cars in the parking lot. So, I attended their Christmas program. I will never forget the physical reaction and the look of almost "terror" on the face of the adult person I sat down next to, after they asked my name. I was a marked man.

Lights from Heaven

I am going to try and explain a third and the wildest experience I have had to date with God and the supernatural realm of the Kingdom of Heaven that is all around us. This happened within the first six months of discovering my new life in God, after the "raw power experience" in my bedroom and the "singing angel choir" at work. My older Brother had recently moved to an apartment in the Portland, Oregon suburb area called Hillsboro. I was still working in the produce department at Fred Myers in North Portland. I contacted him and told him I wanted to come and visit him after work one evening. My relationship was still so fresh with the Spirit of God and I remember as I drove the 20 miles to his apartment after work that day, I was acting like Jesus was riding in the front seat next to me in my car. I was turning and talking to him as I drove.

His Presence was very strong in the car that afternoon and I think I floated out to Hillsboro rather than drove. When I arrived, Rick was watching TV and one of the first things he offered me was to smoke some marijuana. My pattern for the previous three years had been to smoke as much as humanly possible just about anytime and anywhere. I mentioned earlier that I was a cloud of smoke just about everywhere I went, but that night, I said no. This was one of the first times I can remember when I actually turned it down. God's presence was suddenly all I wanted and needed. My brother and I talked briefly and then I settled into staring at the TV screen.

The program we were watching was the detective show called, "Simon and Simon" which consisted of two brothers racing around in a Dodge Charger fighting crime and bandits. I am sure some of you remember the show. (Careful, you're dating yourself!) Anyway, you know how you can fall into an almost "trance" sort of state when you watch TV? I was sitting on the couch watching Simon and Simon do their "thing," when one of the most powerful experiences to date happened to me.

God spoke to me very directly and very forcefully. Suddenly, I found myself with my head tilted up and my eyes staring at the ceiling. This was a direct connection. God wanted my attention and He knew how to get it. This was just like if you did not know someone was directly above you in the room and then they suddenly spoke and said, "Hey Ron, look up here." To say I was surprised and in amazement would be a fairly large understatement. My attention was forcefully grabbed from the TV and I was in a lockdown stare with the ceiling and with Almighty God. I know now that it was His Spirit talking to mine. He left no doubt as He spoke very clearly, commanding me to "Come outside, I have something to show you" and then He gave me control of my head again. I looked down, my mind racing.

The experience was brief, extremely powerful and it shook me. I had been commanded (I don't really think it was a request) to come outside because He was going to show me something. I sat there and looked around for a few seconds trying to catch my breath and process the experience. I knew if I was going to have to get up from the couch and go outside that I should tell my brother sitting on the other end where I was going. The "where I was going" was the easy part, I just could not think of a good reason to explain "why" I suddenly needed to go outside. Anyway, I couldn't wait very long, I knew I had to obey and it needed to be soon. So, I just winged it! I said something like "Ah, I need to go outside to my car, I will be right back". My brother did look away from the TV for a brief second, acknowledged that I had spoken, but then went right back to his "trance" and the program.

As I opened the door of the apartment to go outside, I realized that night had fallen and that it was very dark. I stepped out and closed the door behind me. My car was parked out in the street probably about 20 yards in front of me. I started down the path that led to the street from the apartment walking very carefully, my eyes scanning from left to right.

I remember gravel crunching under my feet. Man, if something would have jumped out at me, I would have had a "batch of kittens" right there. I did not know where to really go because the only instructions I had were to simply, "Come outside, I have something to show you." I reached the sidewalk and my car, yes my 1970 Plymouth Barracuda.

I stood there and looked around for a few seconds and then realized that it was a perfect temperature out that night and that there was an incredibly soft and warm breeze blowing around. Wow, perfect! I calmed down a little and began to relax. I looked up and was instantly captivated by the night sky and a multitude of bright stars. I thought to myself, "This is so cool!" Not given any more specific direction, I decided to slide up on the hood of my car, cross my legs and lean back on the windshield. Similar to my backyard Jr High stargazing days, I put my hands behind my head and started to drink in the incredible view. I am going to have difficulty explaining what happened next.

I came to focus on one particular star for a split second and then it happened. What do you mean, "It happened?" Well, out from behind or from within the star shot this little light. The light acted like it was almost kicked or thrown out and then slowed down a little and began to circle the star that it had just come from. What? I sat up immediately in astonishment and out of unbelief at what I was seeing, then looked down and rubbed both eyes with the back of my hands.

When I looked back up and located the light, I watched as the light got bigger, the circle it was making got larger and then it dawned on me, this thing is coming down at a rapid pace and directly towards me. As I watched this unfold above me, I penned a few good words. Out of my mouth came this, "Oh….. My…… God!" Now, I think at the same time I said these words, I was sliding off the hood of my car coming to rest on my feet in a standing position.

I was trying to position myself better for the incoming phenomenon. When my feet hit the sidewalk beside my car and I came to the end of my "Oh My God" expression, it hit me! It hit me? Yes, it hit me! Now, you might be asking yourself, "What do you mean, what hit you?" A river! A rushing violent river! A rushing violent non-destructive river filled with pure joy engulfed and started flowing through me from head to toe. It was Almighty God in His Spirit form.

I have tried to come up with words to try and explain this and the closest I can come up with is that it was like someone had grabbed me by the hair and was suddenly dunking me up and down in a fast moving Jacuzzi.

As soon as I started experiencing His presence rushing through my body, my hands came together close to my chest and under my chin which was no doubt, my body's reaction to an extremely precious supernatural experience. I could sense teardrops begin to immediately fall from my eyes like I was trying to water the earth! Wow! What happened to the light that was coming down? I watched as it came down and ended up right in front of me head height and about 5 feet away. The light was actually two little lights that were floating in mid-air and kind of jiggling or vibrating back and forth.

I find it interesting when I hear someone talk about time. Time is an interruption in eternity. Almighty God does not live in time. That's why a thousand years can be to Him as a day and a day as a thousand years.

But do not let this one fact escape your notice, beloved, that with the Lord one day is like a thousand years and a thousand years like one day. 2nd Peter 3:8

For a day in Your courts (presence) is better than a thousand outside. I would rather stand at the threshold of the house of my God than dwell in the tents of wickedness.   Psalms 84:10

I brought this time factor up because I was definitely in His presence and in His presence time ceases to exist. So, I have often wondered how long this whole experience lasted that evening. I remember being drawn to prayer one evening years later when I was in the Philippines. I like to find a chair or something comfortable that I can put my knees on the floor, my belly and chest on something soft and my hands in my face.

I arranged some pillows one night in Manila on a hard church pew with my body in the aforementioned fashion and started to praise and give thanks.

Enter His gates with thanksgiving and His courts with praise.   Psalms 100:4

I went deep into prayer that night and when I looked up a little later I had been there for almost three hours! It seemed like only about twenty minutes. But, when you're in His Presence………. anyway, sorry, I will get back to this incredible encounter with God the Holy Spirit on the sidewalk in Hillsboro. To best answer my above question as to, "how long this lasted," I would have to guess no more than two or three minutes, but it's a guess. I do remember at least one car going by because I looked away and was distracted by the headlights for a brief second.

I stood there, hands together against my chest, teardrops falling, watching the little lights in front of me and experiencing this incredible river of love and power race through me from head to toe.

Soon, the little lights disappeared and about 4 feet above and in front of me an open vision appeared. What I saw was Heaven's gates (in color) and the gates were opened wide! Amen! That lasted just a few seconds (maybe) and then another open vision appeared in front of me. This time it was a man's face in silhouette. You know like seeing a face with a light behind it so that you can make out the shape and form and tell it was a man's face. There was not enough light on the face to make out facial features. The Spirit of God told me that this was Jesus' face! That vision went away and I was back to staring at the two little lights that reappeared. I did not know what to do next, curiosity got the best of me and I thought to myself, "The lights are close enough to reach out and touch, I wonder what would happen if I tried?" So, I took a careful step towards them and started to slowly extend my hand in their direction.

To my amazement, the two little lights quickly moved and darted away and to my right about 14 feet and disappeared into thin air. That was amazing, so I said something like, "Wow, come back, come back!" The two little lights reappeared from the same place they had disappeared and came right back in front of me again, about 4 feet away.

I stood there for awhile watching them jiggle and dance back and forth and then I said this, "Come into my heart, I want you in my heart!" At that request, the two little lights slowly started moving towards me. The closer they came to me, the smaller and closer together they became and I watched them disappear into my t-shirt. After that, I stood there dazed for a few seconds and quickly realized that the "rushing violent, non-destructive river, filled with pure joy" that had consumed me had stopped. I tried to catch my breath (kind of like I hope you are right now) and get my mind back under control because it was racing with a thousand thoughts! Whoa! I was back in the present and trying to process what had just happened.

I started to walk back towards the apartment and when I got about halfway there, I began to ask myself, "What am I going to tell my brother Rick? What just happened anyway?" Well, I didn't get a clear answer and I know I was shaking a little as I reached out and turned the door handle.

I opened the door and took a step inside. My brother was distracted from the TV and the "trance" he was in and briefly looked over at me as I stepped in. Then he did something very interesting; he looked back towards the TV and suddenly sat forward from his comfortable position on the couch and took a "double take" looking back at me. I could see the expression on his face and that he had seen and was presently looking at something shocking! I had his attention. I walked towards the couch and began trying to explain what had just happened. I remember sitting down, half pointing in the air, and begin to tell about the lights coming down from the sky when I just lost it! Emotionally, I mean.

I got about 8 or 9 words out and then I just broke down and cried uncontrollably with great waves of emotion still trying to explain what had just happened. I wish I could have known what Rick was thinking. I could tell he was in shock himself and did not know what to do to help me. I asked him a few days later, "When I stepped into the apartment and you sat up and took a double take, was I like glowing?" With some emotion of his own he said, "Yes."

Wow! I had had an apostle Paul like experience with the results of almost needing to wear a veil, like Moses did because of the Glory and Presence of God when he came off of the mountain! I think we need to realize that these great stories and the people in the Bible were actually just like you and I and that God is no respecter of persons. In other words, the ground is level at the foot of the cross and I had better not consider myself something special because of this experience.

The devil jumped all over me right after this and tried to get me to convince myself that I was the second coming, that because of the magnitude of this experience, that I was Jesus Christ in the flesh. For a very brief time, I actually considered it. Thank God, common sense took over and I shook myself out of that delusion and satanic trap. The enemy would have loved to have driven me crazy and given me a new address at a mental institution where I know I would have ended up. Unfortunately, that is the case of many of the precious souls in these institutions, they had incredibly powerful encounters with the spirit realm (most from the dark side) and they had no foundation to stand on that kept them from believing a lie and going "over the edge"!

What Do You Want More Of?

Even though I said "no" to smoking marijuana the night of this incredible visitation, I was still in bondage and was not yet willing to give it up completely. I attended this first church in Gresham for about a year when I had a powerful confrontation and challenge from the Savior. I knew that it was not in my best interest to continue smoking, but the chains/bondage was still in place. I had half-heartedly attempted off and on to quit, but obviously was not ready to give it up. I was simply enjoying it too much. One of the few mornings during the week that I did not get up and smoke right away to start the day was Sunday morning. I would wait to light the joint that I had pre-rolled and was waiting for me in my car as I rolled out of the parking lot at church. As I said earlier, this went on for about a year and then God confronted me with a life changing illustration and question.

God showed me my two hands open and in front of me and said to me, "Ron, put continuing to smoke in one hand and then put getting more of me in the other one. Now, you have to make a choice. You can't have both anymore."

Up to then, I had been growing in my relationship with God and He was showing me that I was now at a crossroads. I realized that I was going to have to make a decision. If I wanted more of Him, more of His presence, more of His guidance, then I was going to have to give up smoking. I had to choose which one I wanted more. I had tried to quit, well sort of, but now I was being faced with having to make a decision, I could not continue living like I was and keep enjoying His presence and have more of Him. I was immediately torn apart. I had tasted of the goodness of God, I was hungering for more of Him, but I was being confronted with my selfishness, my sin and my disobedience.

The Bible talks about great desires that God births in us when we give our lives to Him. Some of them He helps us understand by relating them to something we have no way of misunderstanding and that is to tie them into our taste buds and our bellies! When you taste something good, of course, you want more!

O taste and see that the LORD is good; How blessed is the man who takes refuge in Him. Psalms 34:8

Your words were found and I ate them, And Your words became for me a joy and the delight of my heart; For I have been called by Your name, O LORD God of hosts. Jeremiah 15:16

I had tasted and experienced His Goodness, His Power and His Joy. I knew I was called by His name to do great things. Now, I was being shown that if I chose to continue smoking marijuana that I was not going to get any more of Him, not move forward and that I would not fulfill my destiny and or complete my assignment from Heaven. The painstaking decision was killing me as it drove me to my knees.

I started going to God in prayer and admitting my absolute complete reliance on Him and on His strength alone to get me through the day without being drug off and forced to get high on this stupid weed that grew from the earth.

I was desperate because I knew I had to choose "more of Him" over "continuing to smoke." My life depended on it. The confrontation broke me and as I began to come to God on a daily basis with a sincere desire and with a quality decision to want to be free from this controlling substance, I slowly and surely began to climb up, out and away from this addiction that was threatening the new life that I had found in Him.

I eventually broke completely free and can say today that it is not even a temptation anymore, not a part of my conscience thinking where before, it had controlled and consumed my thoughts. The chain has been broken and I have found freedom in Christ from this controlling substance. Alcohol would be another controlling substance that I struggled with from time to time also, but eventually broke free from as well. God re-imparting His vision and purpose for me in June 2015 would finally be a turning point for that. I will tell you much more on that incredible experience later of God graciously renewing His vision, assignment and purpose for my life. First, we have to get to October 13th, 1993 and we are still in the early 80's!

Two Simons

A few months after finding my greater purpose and new direction, I stopped going to Mt. Hood Community College and moved closer to downtown Portland and a new job. I started visiting a new church downtown and had only gone there a few times when God spoke to me very powerfully during one of the services.

I still am not sure why God did this, but it was powerful and I think I should share it. The preacher during the service was using a passage out of the book of Acts. I don't even remember what he was preaching about, but I do remember that when he got to Acts 10:5-6 and read it, it was like the big building we were all in just cleared out and suddenly, I was the only one there and God was speaking directly to me.

God's Word was quickened to me that morning. Hard to explain, but I believe many of you have had similar experiences. Remember the TV program my brother and I were watching, Simon and Simon?

Now dispatch some men to Joppa and send for a man named Simon, who is also called Peter; he is staying with a tanner named Simon, whose house is by the sea. Acts 10:5-6

You can see why this got my attention that morning! The two Simons are mentioned again later in the same chapter.

Therefore send to Joppa and invite Simon, who is also called Peter, to come to you; he is staying at the house of Simon the tanner by the sea. Acts 10:32

I think that God was just saying "Hello" and wanted me to know He had not forgotten me. I still don't know exactly what to take from this encounter, but that God caused Simon Peter to be invited by a man named "Cornelius" to come to his house and share a message to his friends and relatives.

God used Simon Peter mightily in signs and wonders as he went about preaching to unbelievers. Something I am all about, or want to be!

I love reading the passage in Acts 10:44-45 and can see myself being used in this fashion. Simon Peter had been summoned by some Godly men who had seen Angels in a vision telling them to send for him. When Peter arrived they asked him to tell "all that he had been commanded by the Lord." As he spoke something happened……

While Peter was still speaking these words, the Holy Spirit fell upon all those who were listening to the message. All the circumcised believers who came with Peter were amazed, because the gift of the Holy Spirit had been poured out on the Gentiles also. Acts 10:44-45

I believe God has equipped, appointed, anointed and called me to do things like this. I know my strongest gifts are evangelism, teaching and preaching. To use a hometown NE Oregon term, it's what "cranks my tractor". What "cranks your tractor" or what "starts your engine"? What gets you excited, stirs your passion and jump starts the potential, the assignment and the gifts that Almighty God has placed on the inside of you? Let your presence come Holy Spirit! Fall on us!

One night shortly after this experience, the Holy Spirit moved again confirming these things to me very powerfully and personally. I was reading my Bible and God spoke to me clearly through John 15:16:

You did not choose me, but I chose you and appointed you (arranged ahead of time, equipped for or assigned a job or role to) that you should go and bear fruit and that your fruit should remain, so that whatever you ask the Father in my name, he may give it to you. John 15:16

The Tennis Center

The new job that brought me closer to downtown Portland was being hired as a tennis instructor, office help and grounds keeper at the Portland Tennis Center. The $500 I had spent a few years earlier for the "tennis clinic" in San Francisco had helped me land this new position. I thought it was really cool! The Tennis Center was a 4 indoor and 8 outdoor public facility.

I basically worked for the City of Portland. So there I was, fulfilling my destiny as a player on the professional circuit! Not! There I was, getting to the tennis facility at 6:30AM to open up and put players on the indoor courts, running the court sweeper, teaching tennis lessons and cleaning bathrooms.

One of the early morning players was "Carl" and his group of over 70's plus on court #1 for games of doubles. Carl and his group of friends were amazing! They were faithful two to three times a week players. It seemed like Carl always wore the same street clothes when he would come into play. Along with his attire was a rock necktie, (basically a heavy duty string or small rope with a polished flat rock that would keep it in place under his chin).

I liked talking to Carl and from time to time, one of his buddies would fail to show up so they needed a fourth player on the court. It was a privilege to knock the ball around with them. I hope I can move like that when I hit 70 plus!

One day Carl was downtown Portland wearing his rock necktie and a talent scout from a company in Los Angeles saw him and offered him a spot in a national TV commercial, only if he wore exactly what he had on! I remember him coming into the Tennis Center and talking about his upcoming scheduled trip and flight to Los Angeles for the shoot!

A Man Named "Perry"

I met many different kinds of people at the Tennis Center. One I will never forget is "Perry." Perry walked in one day when I was sitting at the front desk running the cash register and directing players to their court. I had just placed my lunch in front of me on the desk when I looked up and there he was. The first words out of his mouth as he looked at me and then down at my sandwich were, "You going to eat all that?" Perry was homeless, obvious because of the way he was dressed and that his hair was a mess. I found out later that he had been sleeping in the bushes over at a nearby mall. My heart went out to him immediately and I decided that I could go without lunch that day, which made him very happy. He was obviously very hungry. That started a relationship in which I actually invited him to stay with me in my studio apartment not far from the Tennis Center. I tried to help him get back on his feet, but after a few weeks I had to ask him to leave. I can only remember one other person that I had met that was as bitter and angry with his father and immediate family as Perry was. That other man was a homeless person who I met in downtown Portland at the 3rd and Burnside Street "Gospel Mission Outreach" where I first started preaching. Perry, like the other gentleman, was not willing to forgive. He was very bitter towards his father and it was sadly obvious that it was one of the main things that was ruining and controlling his life. After I had to ask him to leave my apartment, I don't think I ever saw him again. I hope you're doing well Perry.

Bring on the "Walter"

I met another gentleman just about the same way. The first time I remember meeting "Walter" was when he came into the Tennis Center and started up a conversation with me. We found out we were both believers so we became instant friends. I admired Walter because he was very bold in his witness for God.

He shared some of his stories of standing on a street corner in downtown Portland and passing out Gospel Tracts and telling people "God Bless You". Many of his stories were of negative reactions to his "gift on display" although it did not seem to bother him at all. I know I really liked talking to him. He was definitely, "out of the box" when it came to a believer. One of the reasons why Walter came into the Tennis Center and I had the pleasure of meeting him was that he was on assignment from God. He came in one day and told me about a new church that he had visited called "New Song". It was close to the Tennis Center and he thought I should go check it out. It seemed reasonable, because any church that Walter would like, I was sure to enjoy myself. God used Walter mightily in providing divine guidance for me, because when I went a few weeks later to the church he suggested, I ran into Jim for the second time. This is an incredible story and I have to tell you about the first time I met Jim. Walter, I hope you're doing well!

Meeting Jim

One of the fun things I got to do for work at the Center was help run tournaments. There is nothing like good competitive tennis going on all around you! I remember standing outside with one of the players as we waited for his opponent (who was running a little late) to arrive. It was a beautiful sunny summer day in Portland and I had a good view of the parking lot when a car came suddenly racing on to the property looking for a parking spot.

The car door opened and out jumped this man with his racquet in his hand. He ran straight towards me, he must have seen the clipboard in my hand and thought I was in charge. He came running up with a look on his face of, "sorry, I know I'm late!" When he got about 20 feet from me, God spoke so clearly and powerfully to me that it took me off guard. The Holy Spirit spoke to me and said, "That man is a Christian."

It was loud and clear. That's all God said, and then I was left to introduce him to his opponent and place them on the right court. I didn't have time for any questions for Jim, as my duties took me quickly away. I remember making a mental note to try and talk to him when he was done with his tennis match, but I never saw him until a few weeks later at another divine encounter.

New Song Church

I was enjoying visiting this new church, "New Song" that Walter had suggested for the first time. It was very "lively" with probably about 800 people there in the service. A man by the name of Richard Probasco had started the church as a small Bible study in his home years earlier and he was still at the helm as Pastor Richard. Richard was very talented, he could sing and played piano which attracted many other talented musicians and singers. I will always remember Pastor Richard as a man that could preach and teach the Word as well. His messages always had practical application to scripture directive. He was also a "hugger" (at 6' 5" height, I came up to his shoulders). At the end of just about every service he would be out near the exit doors hugging all that were willing. It was like being grabbed by a big fuzzy teddy bear! I can't say enough about this man and how God used him to help me and shape me. I will definitely share at least one more story of a meeting we had in his office one day, later.

I don't know about you, but when I would visit a church for the first time my routine was to find a place in one of the back rows so I could "spy out" the land. The singing was going on and then we moved into a transition break, where everyone was shaking hands and greeting each other. I was scanning the crowd in front of me when all of a sudden I saw the man I had briefly met at the Tennis Center a few weeks back, "Jim".

The funny thing is, is that Jim saw me just at about the same time. He obviously recognized me and it was like everyone just cleared out of our way as we searched for a path to each other. It was kind of like the experience that I am sure Moses had when he watched the Red Sea part!

Well, tennis players need each other desperately, so Jim and I became instant friends. This truly was not a coincidence that I ran into Jim that day, there were more than 360,000 people in the Portland area. What were the chances I would see Jim again after the brief Tennis Center introduction. We would become lifelong friends and New Song Church would become my home for the next 13 years, 5 of those years in Portland and 8 more as one of their represented missionaries in the Philippines!

Yes, I had found my home. I have to give thanks to Walter and to Jim for being obedient and allowing God to use them to guide me in to where I would be shaped, loved, corrected and prepared for the future God had for me. I felt called to get involved in just about every ministry that the church was offering. As I said earlier, God had given me a strong voice and I could sing and loved singing.

At the helm of New Songs choir was a multi talented man by the name of Gary Hemenway. Gary was from a small town in NE Oregon like me which was only about 70 miles from Elgin! We had that "small NE Oregon town" connection going on. Gary was also a tennis player. When it came to the piano and music, let's just say Gary knew how to bring some "funk" and "fun" into a group of singers! I auditioned for the choir and was accepted. Wow! I was now a singer in a really cool, rockin' choir. We sang almost every Sunday and would also put on special concerts several times a year.

The next vivid memory I have of New Song was of our full-time youth minister named JT Schulze. I know I had seen him around in the church services and one day he approached me in the "foyer" or front entrance of the building before church and introduced himself.

He then asked if I would pray about coming on and being part of his staff as a volunteer to help with New Songs high school ministry called, "Lightway." I was challenged, so I showed up at youth night during the week and was hooked! I instantly fell in love with the kids. We had weekly youth meetings and I was privileged to go on many overnight youth group "out of town" adventures.

It was on one of these "out of town" excursions that I got to know New Songs main bus driver named, "Larry Robbins". Larry was an Elder in the church, taught a relationship class and had a heart for the kids. Larry also counseled my future wife and I about nine years later before we were married in the Philippines (more of that overseas romance later). Larry would also become a lifelong friend miraculously moving to my hometown Elgin years later where he and his wife, "Billie Jo" still lives today. In Portland, I would be a frequent visitor at their home on the corner of 78th and Everett. Larry and Billie Jo had an open door policy, whoever was hungry or needed encouragement, they were welcome. I remember being amazed when I would visit at the sheer number of people that went in and out of their house. It was as if Larry knew everybody! There were no strangers to him!

Brother Rick Again

After my encounter with the lights from the Heavenlies, my older brother Rick had moved from Hillsboro back to NE Oregon and then back again to the Portland area to attend an accelerated college course in computer programming. Simply put, my older brother is a brain. He currently owns a flourishing Auto Parts Business in hometown Elgin. You don't become a good "parts man" and not be blessed with some intellect. We shared an apartment together in downtown Portland at 20th and Burnside while he was going to school.

Anyway, after graduating from his computer programming course, he tried to secure employment in the Portland area. He had job offers, but was not willing to give up his history to prospective employers because he had had an alcoholic background and had gotten into several brushes with the law. I believe he was convinced that if he shared his past, no one would hire him. In reality, I believe no one would hire him because he was not willing to share his past. I am sure that "shame" was a big reason he was not willing to talk to prospective employers about his history.

When he could not find employment in the computer field, he went back home to NE Oregon and worked for awhile in an auto parts store. Then after about a year he decided to come back again to the Portland area and look again for a career in computers. He was not successful this time either in securing employment and he became very discouraged.

At this point, I think he had been sober for about three years, but he had reached his breaking point. Discouraged over not being able to secure a job in the computer field, married and divorced one time already, an alcoholic for many years, he just reached a point that he did not really want to go on. He decided one evening in Portland that he would "fall off the wagon", drink one last time and then end his life. Da-da-da-da!!!! Enter Ron, his ten speed bicycle and backpack loaded with his Bible! Well, really, enter God to the rescue!

When I was working at the Tennis Center, there was a time when all the wheels I had was a ten speed bicycle. I was in really good shape and remember being able to get around downtown Portland sometimes faster than people in their cars. Anyway, the next morning after Rick had gone out and drank, I felt led by the Holy Spirit to go across town and visit him. So, I loaded my backpack with my thick Dr Ryrie New American Standard Study Bible, got on my bicycle and made the 20 minute ride across the Columbia river to the other side of Portland to Rick's apartment.

When I arrived at his apartment door and knocked for a while and there was no response, I began to smell the strong odor of gas coming from inside his apartment. I hurried down to the managers and let them know. The manager knew me as his brother, so he gave me a key. I went back and opened the door only to find Rick lying on the couch and the room filled with gas. He was awake, he had heard me knocking, but he did not want to see anyone.

He had come home the night before from his "falling off the wagon experience", turned on the gas from his kitchen oven and planned to go to sleep on his couch and not wake up. Thank God his plan did not work. He sat up on the couch when I entered the room and I asked him what was going on. He was really at the "end of his rope" much like myself, just a few years prior.

He went into a tearful brief history of his life saying that he had been such a failure at everything he had ever tried to accomplish. In fact, he said that he had been so unsuccessful in this life, such a "screw up", that he couldn't even do something as seemingly simple as killing himself. He couldn't even do that right. I sat there with him for several minutes at a helpless loss of what to do. He was totally despondent and I knew right away that there was absolutely nothing I could say or do to help him; my only option was to pray for him.

When he finally stopped beating himself half to death right there in front of me with his tearful tirade, I was able to get a few words out in hopes of encouraging him. I said something like, "Well, I hope you have seen the difference in my life, in the changes that have taken place and the help I have received." I did not know what else to do, so I offered a little advice of looking to God for help. I also pulled my Bible out of my backpack and offered to leave it with him if he wanted me to. He agreed and said to "go ahead and leave it". He told me later that the only reason he agreed for me to leave my Bible was that he hoped that after I left it, I would leave and he could go ahead and try and think of another way to end his life.

This reminds me of just a few years earlier that the only reason I agreed to take the little Bible that the young Gideon was offering me on that college campus was that if I took it, maybe he would leave me alone and I would be free to go on my way. So, I placed my Bible on his coffee table in front of him and told him I would come back later and check on him. He said something like, "Sure, whatever". I left, prayed and then came back later that evening. The story is amazing! What happened after I left was a miracle.

Just Try It!

He told me this later, that after I left he sat there on the couch with the Bible in front of him and began to try and think of another way to end his life. He said that as he started to consider various methods that several thoughts kept swooping in and out of his mind. The thoughts were something like, "Just try it" and "Just pick it up, what have you got to lose"? That happened several times before he considered opening up the book in front of him. He didn't realize that God was speaking to him, but after a few times of hearing this suggestion, he decided to open the book, put his finger in the air and come down in a random place. I know he was frustrated and at the same time this was happening, he was asking himself why he could not even accomplish something so seemingly simple as dying. Well, the verse that his finger came down on is found in Ecclesiastes 3:1-2. God spoke to him very powerfully with the answer as to why his death was not already accomplished.

There is an appointed time for everything. And there is a time for every event under heaven—A time to give birth and a time to die; A time to plant and a time to uproot what is planted. Ecclesiastes 3:1-2

Bam! God Spoke to him and answered his question, "Why did I not die last night?" Answer, "Because it was not yet his time."

I came back later that evening to check on him, not knowing for sure what I was going to find. I knocked at his door and immediately heard his cheerful voice say "Come in, the doors unlocked". I walked in and took a look at a completely transformed, different person. There was my brother, sitting on the same couch as he was when I left earlier that morning. He was holding my Bible in front of him open and resting on his legs. He looked up at me and out of his mouth came these words, "This thing is true isn't it?"

I didn't quite know what to say. The obvious outward transformation of his countenance was stunning. He must have been reading my Bible since earlier that morning when God spoke to him. He had been in the presence of God all day and it was obvious. I was on assignment that day and God used me and my thick Dr Ryrie Study Bible to save my brother's life. Oh, what adventure awaits us if we will just make ourselves available.

My Roomy, Paris and My Buddy Bill!

I remember an apartment that I lived at while I was going to New Song and one of my roommates named "Paris." Paris and I had hearts for God, for His Word and for the lost. He used to bring out a stack of Bibles and study books at least a foot high and show me what he was studying.

I think it was the first time I saw a "concordance", which helps you study involving the Greek and ancient Hebrew languages. I love the guy, but one of the things that I still give him a hard time about was his early morning routine that used to get on my nerves. I had never met someone so alive and full of energy in the morning as Paris.

He had a routine of gourmet coffee to start the day and then his peeling of potatoes for hash browns at breakfast. He would often leave his potato peelings in the sink for me to clean up. Then he would brush his teeth before heading out the door to work. He always had to tap his toothbrush on the side of the sink when he was done. I talked to him about the peelings and the noisy tapping in the morning, but it usually went right over his head.

Another one of our friends had met someone at church that needed a place to stay and one afternoon had brought him over to meet us. Paris and I always had room for someone in need. So, one day about 2pm, Bill West from Los Angeles California showed up at our door. For some reason he was in Oregon and needing a place to stay. Bill and I sat down in the hallway of our apartment and started to talk.

I had never found it so easy and enjoyable to talk to someone. Pretty soon I looked around and noticed that it was starting to get dark. I looked at my watch and found out that Bill and I had been talking for almost 3 hours. Becoming instant friends, Bill was someone that I would also stay in contact with for the rest of our lives. Unfortunately, Bill's life would end at the early age of 50. He was an avid bicycle rider and would be run over from behind a few years ago as he started out on a coast to coast USA trip. I am really looking forward to seeing Bill again.

The Call Was Still There

In all, I lived in Portland and attended New Song for about 5 years. The call, leading and desire to go around the world and spread the Gospel of Jesus and His Kingdom, this new life, was still there and only growing stronger. I asked God many times how this was going to happen and what was the "vehicle" He was going to use to take me around the world and when? God was preparing me and most of the time I was patient, trusting in His timing and purpose.

My volunteer involvement with New Song consisted of singing in the choir, staff with the high school ministry and an active participant on the street evangelism team. The street evangelism team is where I met "Duane" the first time, more on Pastor Duane later, believe me, it's a miracle! What's next? Well, many things as this was still just the beginning.

I had another amazing experience that I have to tell you about. This was exciting! God's timing had come and it was time to show me the "vehicle" I was to ride in to go around the planet. I came to church one Sunday only to find out that we had a visiting ministry team in charge of the service. In all, I think there were about 10 team members and they were missionaries from all over the world.

I will never forget one of them from Russian descent because I had never seen anyone do that Russian dance that only they can do. You know the one where you're squatting, arms folded out in front of you and jumping back and forth from one foot to the other. Then I remember two or three girls in traditional Holland dress dancing and spinning down the aisles to music and throwing little flowers out into the crowd from baskets they held in front of them! Wow! I was enamored and on the edge of my seat!

Right in front of me, access to the whole world opened up and God showed me that this was a ministry that I needed to find out more about. How and where do I sign up!

Because God spoke to me so powerfully, I would have left with them after the service if they would have allowed it. But, alas, after talking to them, I found out you have to actually go through a short missionary training school and then you could join a traveling ministry team and go on an "outreach" like they were doing that day.

Thank you Lauren Cunningham for being obedient to the call and the vision God gave you of a multitude of young people going to the nations like ocean waves crashing on shores, because it was that day that one of your "YWAM" teams came to New Song. I found out that there was a "Youth With a Mission" school and training base in nearby Salem, Oregon which was only an hour drive from Portland! This is where someone interested in short and long term missions could get started. They offered a program called a "DTS" or Discipleship Training School that was the first step to becoming a missionary! The school consisted of a three month lecture and training phase on base where you lived in community with other staff and students. After the lecture phase, the students and staff would be divided up into smaller groups and go on short term (usually two month) outreaches that went to various parts of the world, basically a 5 to 6 month program in all.

I had found the vehicle that God was going to use to take me to my destiny. I thought I was ready to go but God still had a little more molding for me to go through, although it would not be long after this initial contact with the YWAM team. About nine months later, I was still working with JT and the high school ministry. In the summertime we would move our weekly youth night outside to a nearby park and set up a stage and sound equipment. I remember very clearly one late afternoon when we were having our youth function in the park.

The Presence

At the youth meeting that afternoon, I was throwing a Frisbee around with some high school students before we started when JT's voice came over the speaker system announcing we were about to begin the meeting. So, we all began walking and jogging back to the stage area.

As I jogged over and made it about halfway back to the stage, God spoke ever so clearly to me. I will never forget it. He said, "In the fall, your life is going to change!" It was like Heaven opened up all around me and I knew right away what that meant. The YWAM DTS in Salem started in the fall and by faith, I started making concrete plans to be there in September.

Later that summer, I gave notice to the Portland Tennis Center that I was quitting and moving. The YWAM base was only a one hour drive south to Salem. I said goodbye to all my precious friends at New Song and loaded my little yellow Datsun pickup.

I was zealous in my "turning away" from the things of this world. Things like the superficiality of dedicating myself to the sport of tennis "just to see how good I could get" and the attitude and mentality of some of those that could afford to play the sport who also belonged to expensive indoor clubs. I felt that it was time for me to turn my back on this world and dedicate myself to a much higher calling. I was ready to lay down my racquet and go for God!

I remember all my earthly possessions that I kept (my tennis racquet included, which I had laid down but not forgotten where I had put it) fit inside the cab and the canopy that I had on the back of my little pickup.

I will never forget the feeling of the incredible, never before felt freedom as I drove the hour from Portland to Salem. I was available and I could literally go anywhere in the world, nothing tying me down!

YWAM Base, Salem Oregon

I remember turning and driving onto the YWAM base ready to check in for the 5 month Discipleship Training School. As I turned off Battlecreek Rd SE onto the property there in South Salem, I sensed the presence of God and the excitement of the Holy Spirit over these 75 acres. A sense of destiny was all around me. There were about 8 or 9 separate buildings that consisted of a cafeteria, classrooms, offices, several different types of dormitories, a large meeting hall, a prayer tower and maintenance buildings. A small creek ran through the middle of the property. It was all so majestic and the best thing is that there were about 75 people, students and staff that I had never met!

I moved into the "single guys" dormitory and a top bunk with about 17 other new found friends from different parts of the US and a few from international locations. This place was a greenhouse for spiritual growth! I remember our days being structured with just about every minute needing to be somewhere, busily doing something. I remember hurriedly writing letters to my parents on 20 minute breaks during the day. We were assigned work crews to be on during this 3 month lecture phase of the school. I ended up on the "firewood crew" which consisted of a group of guys cutting and delivering firewood to most parts of the campus and buildings for heating purposes.

Classroom time was two hours in the mornings from 10am to 12 noon five days a week. Guest speakers from all over the country came and taught us Biblical principles and told incredible stories of evangelism and how God had led them all over the world to do powerful things that touched a multitude of lives. Many of the stories included the fact that they did not have the money to go on these adventures, and God would supply sometimes at the last minute as they stepped out in faith and obedience! For me, this was a completely new culture, a new way of thinking that challenged me, but rang true in my heart.

I was learning about this "YWAM" and that it was an international organization that offered these DTS's and other training schools all over the world. They have an international central hub in Kona, Hawaii where they have their largest training base that is a launching point for thousands of short and long term missionaries. These trained missionaries literally go to the ends of the earth. The possibilities were seemingly endless as to where I could go and what God might have in His mind and heart for me.

Our First Instructor

I have to tell you about the first week of classroom lecture and Bible training. There was a gentleman that actually lived on the base in his own separate house who was our teacher for the first three days of classes. His name was Duane Rawlens. I soon discovered that Duane was not only a Bible teacher, but he was also a businessman, a real estate agent and part owner of an indoor tennis club in downtown Salem. You're probably ahead of me by now, yes, out came the racquet! It was funny because I was so determined to give up the game and go for God and here God was saying, "Play on!"

Duane taught me and my fellow classmates on the subject of, "Bible Meditation." I had never heard anyone teach on this subject. Duane was in his second marriage but he spoke ever so fondly of his first wife that had previously passed.

He took us through the great emotion of losing her and how he hoped that when he was gone, his children would not fight over any finances left, but that they would wrestle for possession of his late wife's Bible that he showed us in class. This Bible was where his late wife would meet with God on a daily basis and I could tell that it was one of his, if not the most valuable possession that he owned.

One of the scriptures that Duane shared with us was found in Ps 119:103;

How sweet are Your words to my taste! Yes, sweeter than honey to my mouth! Psalms 119:103

I remember him talking about comparing Bible Meditation to the pleasurable experience of your first juicy kiss! At first his statement kind of seemed controversial, should kissing even be mentioned in Bible class? There were a lot of young people in the classroom that were not married! Hmm.....never heard that before, but it did ring true and stir up in me an incredible desire to be away with my Bible and the Holy Spirit in private intimate relationship.

Duane told us if we did not like the word "honey" from Ps 119:103 then it was ok with God to put something in there that we did like, like "Pizza!" How sweet are your words to my taste, yes, sweeter than pizza to my mouth! Wow! Never had heard that either! Duane was amazing.

Outreach Phase

About half way through the three month lecture and training phase of my DTS we started talking about the opportunities for the outreach phase of the school which usually lasted two months. We had three possibilities or options for this part of the school and we were asked to pray and ask God which team we thought we were to commit to.

The first opportunity we learned about was a puppet team that would travel to Mexico. The second was an evangelistic team that would fly to Jamaica for their two month outreach.

The third was a children's ministry drama team called, "Jacob's Ladder" that would stay in the States. The Ladder team required not a two month commitment after the lecture phase, but six months. Three of the six month commitment was traveling on a yellow school bus, touring and ministering on our way to New York City and back. While on tour, the Ladder team would stop and stay with host homes and minister in churches all the way to the East coast, perform and minister to children in New York City parks for three weeks and then another schedule of churches to stop at on the way back to Oregon and the West coast.

The staff of the DTS met with us weekly to pray about which direction we thought God was leading us. I remember watching a video one day in class of a former Jacob's Ladder team. Here were these youth along with grown men and women, about 10 of them, all in costume and makeup, dancing around to music and interacting with one another.

This was a farm setting with a barn that had a puppet window with curtains that was pulled back when it was time for the puppets to act out a story. I was amused! Here was their leader called, "Jacob" (in bright yellow overalls, pink cheeks and floppy farmers hat) who owned this farm with some animals on it. "Gerdie the Goat", "Clea the Cat" and "Pamela the Pig" add "Grandpa and Grandma", Jacob's sister "Jenny" and of course the bad guy called, "Scarecrow" and you had the cast. There was also the sound man and two puppeteers that were behind the scene.

The animals on Jacob's farm all had problems that Jacob would actually climb and sit up on a five foot ladder and talk to God about. Jacob always came down off the ladder with the solution. It seems that Gerdie the goat was selfish and did not want to share her toys, Clea the cat was scared all the time and Pamela the pig did not like the way God had made her.

As we were watching that video of the former Jacob's Ladder team in class that morning, I distinctly remember elbowing a classmate next to me, quietly laughing out loud and saying something like, "You'll never catch me doing anything like that!" I was confident that God had answered my prayer and that His direction for me was to head overseas to Jamaica to preach the Gospel! That was it! I was going to be this "international guy" and it was a plane ticket for me!

At this point, I have to laugh out loud again! The school staff did not seem to understand because they kept asking me if I had prayed about the outreach team I was to commit too. I had told them it was Jamaica for me, but they did not seem satisfied and kept asking me, "If I was sure?"

Well, when I actually took the time to open my heart and my mind to the possibility that God just might want me on the Jacob's Ladder team and really prayed about it, an amazing thing happened. It became so obvious and clear that I had allowed myself to be misguided by my own ambitions. Not only did I end up on the "Ladder" team but I landed the lead role getting to wear yellow overalls, pink cheeks and a floppy farmer's hat!

Because of the extended time of committing to the "Ladder" team my finances were not going to be sufficient to cover it. I wrote a few letters and one of them was to the missions board and the Elders at New Song Church in Portland. I was letting them know what my plans were and where I believed God was leading me.

I also let them know about my financial situation and asked if they would pray and consider supporting me. I was thrilled when they and others responded positively with a small amount of monthly financial help for the duration of the outreach phase.

Our team worked very hard memorizing lines and putting together choreography for about 6 weeks after the school portion had ended before we had our first performance. We ended up with four 30 minute programs which included drama, singing, dancing and puppets.

Each program was centered around a problem on the farm and Jacob going up the ladder to talk to God and find the solution. Miraculously, God would come through every time! We ministered in a few churches locally before we loaded the bus for the 3 month tour to New York City and back. We would usually drive for a day or two and then we were at our next church, our next host homes to stay at for a few days and our next round of programs and ministry to children and families.

Then we would load the bus back up and drive again for another day or two and do it all over again. When we were in New York City for three weeks, we set up in city parks almost every day and ministered to the kids, adults and families that happened to be there. I distinctly remember having to keep a watchful eye on some of our equipment so it did not get up and walk away! I had never been to New York and I thought it strange that some people wanted to steal our stuff! Didn't they know we were there to help them!

After our three weeks in the city parks of New York, we started our schedule back across to the West coast stopping and ministering at different churches along the way. When we finally arrived back in Salem after being on the road for three months, I was never so happy to get off of a yellow school bus in my life.

As a team, we had a great time and I am still in touch with some of the cast almost 30 years later. But, when you put 10 people together for that long in a bus doing ministry over and over, eventually conflicts arise and personalities clash! We were like "Iron Sharpening Iron" and sometimes sparks flew (mostly from me)!

Back to Portland

The team dispersed and we all went our separate ways. "Grandpa" and my sister "Jenny" eventually married and are Pastors in Salem today. The "Scarecrow" and "Clea" the cat were already married and went on to open their own successful accounting firm and they are also still in Salem today. I am not sure where everybody else is right now. We have talked about getting together someday for a reunion.

I did not have any specific direction of where to go after the outreach so I went back to Portland and New Song Church. I landed a delivery driving job with "Best Buy Bark Dust" located at the intersection of Canyon Blvd and Hwy 217. I drove a 6 wheel dump truck all over the West side of Portland and delivered sand, gravel, bark dust and firewood to residential homes. I plugged back into church trying to catch my breath from my grueling schedule as a traveling actor and singer with the "Ladder" team.

I was back in Portland for about a year when I started inquiring into YWAM again about attending another training school. The "Biblical Counseling School" in Kona, Hawaii was very similar in structure to the DTS that I had completed in Salem, but what caught my attention was not so much wanting or desiring to become a "counselor," but that the destination of the outreach phase was the Philippines and that caught my attention and excited me.

I was not satisfied with just working and making a living. The call of God back in high school was not going away nor was it fading. I knew I had to get to the Philippines and this looked like a viable option to obtain that goal. I started making plans to soon leave New Song behind, again. I will never forget one of the next events that happened as I prepared to leave.

In The Man's Office!

Pastor Richard heard of the news as I had told various people around the church what my plan was for the coming fall. One day, I received a phone call from Richard and he wanted to meet with me in his office. We made an appointment and I came in one morning to see him. I had only been alone with Richard one other time that I can remember and that was on a racquetball court. In the heat of competition that day, I remember there had been a discrepancy in the score and with both of us being competitors, well, I felt kind of bad at the way we parted. Anyway, that was all in the past and forgotten about as we met together a second time alone.

I sat down in one of the chairs in front of his big desk and we began to talk. He told me he had heard that I was planning another adventure with YWAM to Hawaii and then possibly to the Philippines. He shared his concern for me that he thought it would better serve me if I just stayed in Portland, continued to plug into the church and continued to grow emotionally and spiritually. I know his concern was sincere and that he had my best interests in mind.

At this point, I have to laugh out loud again! I need to share with you briefly one of the reasons (and a good one) why Pastor Richard was thinking this way. You see, a few years earlier there had been a certain young lady in the church that I had begun to start a relationship with. We had played tennis once and had started to sit together at church. I will never forget one service when I looked down and to my left at her. She looked up at me and when our eyes met briefly, I had an explosion of emotion that just completely engulfed me. It was so powerful that I had to close my eyes and look up and away.

I literally thought I was going to bounce off the ceiling during this experience in church that day. I think one day I will be able to write a book on the power of our emotions. I had never experienced anything like that before. I was completely overwhelmed and speechless. Long story short, I allowed my emotions after this experience to completely control me and cause me to look like an idiot. Of course, I had to share with her that "she was the one" and that we were to be married! Big mistake because she was just getting comfortable with us being friends and my confession caused her to react opposite to what I thought should happen. Basically, the friendship was over and it was my fault for not displaying a little more self-control. Anyway, Pastor Richard had to graciously step in and give me some very strong council that helped save my life because I could not stop the roller coaster of emotions I was experiencing. She really did not want anything to do with me after that. I am sure I had frightened her. Anyway, I am sure Pastor Richard was thinking along these lines when he counseled me that day in his office to stick around and mature.

Back in his office, I sat there and listened intently to what he was saying. As he talked and tried to convince me that I should stay and not leave, something on the inside of me started to stir, build and rise up (I know now that most of that was just raw, powerful emotion). Pretty soon I could not sit and take it any longer, I had to stand up and interrupt him. I stepped towards him, leaned over and put both of my hands flat on his desk and said, "Richard, don't you ever get the urge to go?" I could tell by his physical reaction that he was probably thinking something like, "Help, there is a crazy man in my office!" I'm sure I was lit up! When I stepped towards him and said that, he went silent, leaned back in his chair and his eyes got about the size of quarters. Our meeting was coming to an abrupt end! I know he could tell that there was absolutely nothing he could say at this point to try and get me to see things his way. I was bent on getting to the Philippines and a team of white, wild horses would not have been able to hold me back!

After I leaned over his desk and asked him, "don't you ever get the urge to go" and he could speak again, he said something like this, "Well……..uh…….., Yes I do" and then he said after a short pause, "Ok……. if that's how you feel, (And boy did I) then don't expect anything from the church in the form of financial support." When he said that, I just about lost it (I was already halfway there anyway). I had not come into his office that day to ask for money and I let him know how I felt about it. Man! I wish I had that meeting captured on video! It would be priceless! Richard, thank you for putting up with me! This is Interesting though, when I did get to the Philippines and needed financial support, New Song stepped up and was my biggest supporter!

Preparing For Hawaii

Who doesn't want to go to Hawaii! Come on! I started making preparations for my next YWAM School which needed to be paid for before I left. I had a little money saved and I sold my Datsun pickup to help come up with the rest to cover the school and the plane ticket to Kona. I would have to believe God for more finances for the outreach phase to the Philippines. I was so excited! I was on my way to fulfilling my destiny and the direction I had received back in my high school hallway of God's presence and the overwhelming desire to go to the Philippines! God had planted and was stirring up a seed in me that had continued to grow for the last eight years and now I was about to see and experience the fruit of it. This was the fall of 1988 and the Biblical Counseling School or "BCS" started in September.

I packed my thick Dr. Ryrie Study Bible, my tennis racquet, a few clothes and said goodbye to my friends at New Song again. Awesome! Off to another adventure and mission! I remember the memorable four hour plane ride as we got closer to the Hawaiian Islands and the time for "airplane aerobics."

As the flight to Hawaii was almost complete and we started to descend, they started showing a "workout" video" over the media system and big screens on the airplane. Maybe you have seen it; lift one arm, now both, run in place while sitting etc.... What was awesome was that there were beside myself, only one other person that I could see in front of me that was participating in the jam-packed airplane.

He turned to see if there was any other "crazy" person beside himself participating and that's when this stranger and I made eye contact and celebrated our fearless, unashamed love for the workout. We didn't care if we were being ignored or what other people thought, we were going to enjoy our descent. We were probably both first timers to the islands! I know I was!

After we landed in Kona, I headed for the YWAM campus and to touch base with some of my fellow students of the BCS. The school was going to be another three month classroom lecture and training phase and then a two month outreach to the Philippines. We soon discovered that we were to live and go to school at the extension campus north on the island called "Maka Pala" which was about a forty-five minute drive from Kona.

A staff member picked us up at the airport and drove us up there in a van. This was a part of the island that was untouched by commercialism. It was tropical, very close to the end of the road and so fresh and clean!

The campus base was very similar to the one in Salem with staff and students living in community. I settled into the guys dorm and we started hearing right away about the beaches and riding the waves or "boogie boarding" which was something I had never tried. That was definitely on my priority list of things to experience while I was there.

I also had actually come to the island with a contact that was in the tennis teaching profession at one of the 5-star resorts in Kona. It was the relative of a friend at New Song in Portland. I planned on touching base with him while I was there and play a little tennis. School started a few days after we arrived with about 20 students which was a little smaller than my DTS in Salem.

I will never forget one of the schools teachers that travels all over the world, authors books and teaches on the "Father Heart of God". In YWAM circles, he is a bit of a Legend! His name is "Floyd McClung" and I remember him as a soft spoken man as he taught the five days or one week that he was assigned. I had an incredibly amazing experience with the Holy Spirit and God's Father Heart during class time that week that I have to tell you about.

The Father's Heart

Floyd had been teaching for 3 or 4 days when during class this particular day, we took some time to seek the Father's Heart in prayer. I consciously remember leaning forward in my chair, putting my elbows on my knees, hands together with head down and eyes closed. Floyd was praying over the class and leading us in seeking God's heart. We had only been in prayer for a minute when I became physically aware that I was gently rocking back and forth from side to side in my chair. When I became aware of the motion, I thought it was odd because it was something I had not consciously begun on my own. The experience was very comforting so I allowed it to continue and just "went with it".

Shortly after I became aware of the rocking motion, I was suddenly transformed by the Holy Spirit into an infant that was being held in a loving embrace by God the Father. I was suddenly on my back (in the Spirit) and looking directly up and into a smiling face above me. It was a vision of Father God.

He held me close just like you would hold a newborn, rocking them back and forth in your arms while looking down with adoration and love. My heart melted and I turned into warm butter right there and then! I can't put into words what this intimate experience and revelation of God's Heart as His precious child did for me.

To know and experience God's love in such an intimate setting was life changing and I am sure something that I needed deep down in my soul and spirit. It is something that everyone on the planet needs to experience. This intimate relationship with God is something we lost in the garden when we disobeyed God. It makes me think of how many countless people are walking around the planet today and they don't know that there is a Father in Heaven and that He loves them just like you love or would love your first born and hold them tight.

This is a message for all the fatherless children in the world that have grown up and are now in prison for crime and violence. Many so called, "good people" in the church are also lacking this awareness and experience of how God really loves us like a caring Father; not like the sperm donor and that abandoned them.

See how great a love the Father has bestowed on us, that we would be called children of God; and such we are. 1st John 3:1

Beloved, let us love one another, for love is from God; and everyone who loves is born of God and knows God. The one who does not love does not know God, for God is love. By this the love of God was manifested in us, that God has sent His only begotten Son into the world so that we might live through Him. In this is love, not that we loved God, but that He loved us and sent His Son to be the propitiation for our sins. 1st John 4:8-10

That was a very powerful experience that I had with the Holy Spirit that day as God revealed His Father's Heart for me. I know until just the last few recent years, my earthly biological father had been unable to share his emotions because he'd come from the "men just don't do that" group and mentality. He too is one of the walking wounded that needs this revelation so he can be free also to share his emotions. As I write this and pray for him, he is just past his 86th birthday. God Bless You Dad, I love you!

Time to Boogie!

Enough of this emotional classroom stuff! It was time to hit the beach! After all, I was in Hawaii! Some of the braver (or just plain crazier) guys in my school and I began exploring the beaches. We bought ourselves 3 foot surf boards called "Boogie Boards" and started to try and ride the waves! With a set of flippers or swim fins to help propel you, we would lie on our boards in the surf and try kicking furiously to catch a wave for a short ride. We were successful from the start and thought we were just pretty darn good although we all grew up far from beaches and anything like this.

I remember one day when the islands were experiencing a tropical storm. I was standing high above the surf on a hill and watching the "sets" of waves rolling in, captured by how majestic and powerful they were. The storms would last several days and the waves were probably three to four times the size that they normally were. You guessed it, a group of three of us went to our favorite boogie boarding beach during one of these storms. I stood there and watched these massive waves roll in one after another. The faces of these waves would reach from about 15 to 20 feet in height. The power of these beasts as they rolled in and crashed on the beach just in front of us stirred something primal, dangerous and incredibly risky in me.

We noticed that way out in the surf was one lone surfer that was participating and I wanted desperately to give it a go with my boogie board and flippers, but none of my buddies that day felt like risking their lives. They were smart to want to stay on the beach when all of a sudden; one of the locals appeared with his boogie board and prepared to get in the water. I saw my chance! I would just follow this guy out and do what he did!

So off I went into the unknown. It did not take long to get to where the waves reached way over my head. I was watching the fellow in front of me and how he handled himself when the waves started to "top" and crash down on him. It looked like he actually would leave his board on the surface and dive under the wave as it crashed over the top of him.

This way he was able to get past the wave and push out into deeper water further out. So, that's what I did, just before this massive wave topped over on me, I slipped off my board and dove under the crashing wave.

What I did not realize is that by leaving my board (that was tied to my ankle by a small rope) on the surface allowed the crashing wave to rip the rope right off my ankle and take my board all the way into the beach where my friends stood speechless! When I came up for air and saw that my board was no longer with me, I had just about another 5 seconds before the next monster wave crashed down on me.

I remember thinking how helpless I would have been if not for the flippers on my feet which helped me stay on the surface when I wasn't ducking the next crashing wave. Well, I thought to myself, no choice but to head back to the safety of the beach now. I started back and found it easy going until I got about 25 yards from the beach. I had never experienced "undertow" before and it was that day we were introduced.

Because the waves were so big and so much water was rushing up onto the beach, the returning water back to the deep blue was like a river running from the beach back into the ocean. This causes what is commonly called, "undertow," and the only way to get to the beach when you're in this type of water was to ride the waves with your board on top of and over the returning water. But, alas, I had no board and found myself neck deep in water. My board was safely on the beach as well as my buddies who I could tell did not want to come into the water to try and help me.

I was doing fine swimming toward the beach until I ran into the river trying to return to the ocean. I quickly realized that no matter how hard I swam towards the beach, that the undertow was much stronger and I was not able to go any further. After about the second or third time I tried to swim in and failed, I realized that the current was also taking me down the beach where the waves were crashing into some very jagged and dangerous rocks. So, about the second time I swam back up parallel to the beach and away from the rocks, I began to get completely exhausted.

My body became numb even though I was in the best shape and condition of my life. I haven't told you about how much I had been running since I had arrived in the islands. I was a long distance runner and I had never experienced the distance and pace I was setting while there at the school.

This Is It! Time To Go!

So, to feel this exhausted and out of breath was new territory. My schoolmates on the beach did not know what to do, even though they could see my plight and heard my cries for help. It was then that I had another incredible experience with God. My circumstances and the reality of the conditions I found myself came crashing in.

I came to the conclusion that I was not going to make it back to the beach and that this was it, I was going to drown right here, right now! I saw no way back to the beach and I accepted the fact that I would not touch land again in this life. Amazing what goes through a person's mind just before seemingly inevitable death.

Once I had accepted my plight, I had the strangest peace and calm come over my entire being. I just relaxed, realized that this was it for this earthly life and accepted it. I knew that I knew where I was headed. Death at that moment did not scare me as God's supernatural peace completely overcame me and a confidence from another realm gently flooded my soul.

I was ready! I did have one regret though that came to me, I knew that my mother was going to be heartbroken when she was told the news that I had drowned. Yes, at that moment, I was thinking about my Mother! Brought into the world in water and then taken out of the world in water!

What happened next is the reason I am still here to put this on paper. Whether he was the "boogie boarder" that I had followed out minutes earlier into the surf or an angel, I don't know for sure, but over my right shoulder I heard someone say, "Hey, do you need some help?"

I turned to see what looked like the young man I had followed out into the surf. He still had his board and was offering help. He seemed a little irritated, like I had interrupted his fun and that he was getting tired of saving the lives of stupid mainlanders that came out here and did not know what they were doing.

Well, I wanted to live, I really did not want to die yet, so I said, "yea man!" So, with both of us holding onto his styrofoam boogie board and kicking like crazy, we were able to work our way with the help of the incoming waves pushing us up and over the returning rushing river of undertow, safely back to the beach.

I am sure I said "thank you" but I don't remember much about the next few minutes as I sat there on the beach with my head between my knees, trying to catch my breath. As I sat there my life flashed before my eyes. I don't know why, but it just did. There really is something about a near death experience!

I sat there for about 10 minutes until I regained my strength. Then I did something that still kind of shocks me when I think about it today. I was told growing up that if you're riding a horse and he bucks you off, the best thing you can do is get right back on so fear does not control you the rest of your life and you never ride another horse. You're probably ahead of me, yes, I grabbed my board and went back out! This time determined not to let go of it.

I had discovered somehow that the surfer I had followed out earlier had not let go of his board and swam under the surf when the wave crashed down, he had actually pushed the nose of the board down under the surface with his head and shoulders right behind it allowing the rushing water of the wave to go over the top of his body which allowed him to move on out further to deeper water. He had not let go of it and swam under the surface like I had done just a few minutes earlier.

It worked! I was actually making my way out far enough that I thought it was time to turn around and finally catch one of these "babies" and see what it was like to ride a twenty foot wave! What was it like? I will tell you what it was like! It was like going from 0 to 60 in two seconds flat because I suddenly found myself going straight down the steep face of this massive wave that yes, I was riding! The ride was so bumpy that I knew nothing but a death grip on the board would keep it securely under me. It was an unchartered, blood thinning experience that lasted about 4 seconds (maybe 5) before the wave topped and thousands of gallons of sea water came crashing down on top of me.

In that moment, I remembered my note to self when I went out this second time which was, "Don't let go of the board!" I remember being tossed around like a rag doll in a front loading washing machine and somehow I had gotten not only my arms but my legs wrapped around the board as well and I was holding on for, to coin a phrase, "dear life." I popped back up to the surface with board in hand and said to myself, "It's time to get back to the beach because I am in over my head!" It was not the pleasant smooth experience that I thought it would be. I had seen surfers ride massive waves on TV and it looked easy and fun. This was violent and one wave was enough! I made it triumphantly back to the beach, not letting the surf get the best of me.

Christmas Break

The classroom portion of the school came to an end and most of the students and staff was preparing to go home for the almost 3 week Christmas break until after the first of the year when the outreach phase would start. I remember not having enough money to fly home for the holiday, so I would be one of the skeleton crew still left at Maka Pala to "man the fort." I didn't even have enough money to buy a ticket to the Philippines, let alone pay for my planned 2 month outreach there. So, I went job hunting. I walked up onto a few construction sites where homes were being built and quickly landed a position sanding boards with an electric sander. Pretty lucky really, jobs on the islands I was told later were in short supply.

I had made contact in Kona with the tennis instructor I told you about earlier. Somehow, I had made the 45 minute trip to Kona several times to play tennis with him. I also put myself on a list at the resort and made myself available to play with hotel guests as they flew in and out of the islands. The resort was a 5 star place and they treated you like royalty.

I remember girls coming out to the tennis courts making sure we had enough cold water to drink and fresh towels to wipe our sweat. I had also made contact with a business owner who offered me a position with his company. This opportunity came as a great distraction and temptation to not get on that airplane for the Philippines. He owned a dive shop and scuba diving business taking wealthy travelers out diving. (Remember my first year in college when I took a scuba diving class and earned my certification?)

Wow! I had a vision; there I was in my 12 foot rubber boat, hat turned backwards, wearing sunglasses, extremely tanned and brown from all the sun, cruising out to nearby reefs to take wealthy, international travelers diving. After the dive, maybe a little tennis at the 5 star resorts! Come on Baby! I had arrived! I mean seriously! All this, and Heaven too!

It was something that I considered long and hard and my heart was being torn apart. I knew what God had brought me to the islands for which were the school and a temporary stop before reaching my destiny and assignment of going to the Philippines. It would have been very easy to stay and play, but I had to answer the call of God. It was not an easy decision and I actually had to borrow money from my parents, going into debt to pay for the airfare to Asia. I turned my back on Hawaii and soon found myself strapped into the seat of another big jet, this time headed to a greater unknown than just Hawaii.

When I finally got settled into my plane seat with my seatbelt securely fastened, I had an experience I will never forget. This was different than boarding the plane a few months earlier on my way to Hawaii. Suddenly, I was strongly tempted to panic, jump up and say, "Ah, excuse me, but I think I made a mistake getting on this plane." I was suddenly wrestling with an unknown fear and a slight panic attack. I had never really experienced it like this before.

The realization that once in the air, there was just no guarantee that I would ever make it back to the States again, and that was almost overwhelming. "Besides", I thought to myself, "I didn't even have enough money to pay for this."

It was a sinking feeling, but I had made up my mind. I was going to make it to the Philippines or die trying. I centered myself, took a couple of deep breaths, re-adjusted the seat belt and said something like, "To go where no man has gone before!" "Star Trek" was definitely one of my favorite television programs that I used to watch when I was younger! Sorry for the drama, I was headed to the other side of an unknown world and did not know if I would ever make it back. This was not just a short, festive trip to known Hawaii.

Are Those Clouds?

Eighteen hours later, we came down in our approach for landing in Manila, Philippines. I noticed out the small airplane window that I could see city lights and that we were breaking through what I thought were clouds on our way down. I found out later that those were not clouds; it was smog we were breaking through.

We taxied to the terminal and the plane came to a stop. I gathered my things, tired from not being able to sleep very much during the 18 hours of flying and headed to the exit door. I will never forget the wall of heat and humidity as I stepped out of the plane that greeted me inside the airport. What was this? It was like being thrown into a furnace or walking into an oven. The air was heavy and it was hot!

I didn't know it, but there must have been about 3 or 4 other short term missionaries on that same flight because we were all gathered up by one of the staff from the YWAM base, put on an open, non-air-conditioned sort of vehicle type thing, and started the hour long trip across Manila to the city of Capitolio, Pasig in East Manila, where we would call home for a few months.

I was in amazement at what I saw as soon as we got away from the airport. The time was around 1 o'clock in the morning and there were people literally everywhere! I had never seen so many people. They were in the street, all over the sidewalks, what was everybody doing? I remember the staff member looking at us and being slightly amused as she could tell what we were experiencing for the first time. We had just landed in the middle of about 14 million people that made up Metro Manila. This was a bit of a shock for a guy that grew up in a 1,600 person town. Even living in Portland for five years did not compare with this. What in the world was I doing here in this strange and distant land? Could this really be God?

The Counselling Base and "Pineda"

It was time to meet the team. I had new friends from New Zealand, Japan, Europe and of course the good old USA. There were about 12 of us that were to live in one of two big houses that made up the YWAM Counseling base. We would eat breakfast at our house and then a short walk for lunch and dinner at the other home.

Our home was in a very nice neighborhood but only about 4 to 5 blocks away was the polluted Pasig River and a congested and crowded squatter area called "Pineda." Pineda was where I would begin to pour out my life and heart in ministry. The base had an outreach to Pineda that started with a Monday through Friday morning children's feeding program. We would get up early, cook different types of a breakfast porridge which mainly consisted of rice and then head out to Pineda. It would take at least two of us because we would cook the breakfast in a big cast iron pot, use a towel to wrap around the handles because of the heat and then walk the distance to Pineda carrying the hot breakfast. We carved out a route through the squatter area trying to find the families that had the greatest need with the most children.

It was hard for me to understand how people could live in these types of conditions. Congested squatter areas are littered all over Manila, hundreds of them. These areas mostly consisted of people that had moved into Manila from outlying areas in hopes of finding employment. The living conditions were bad. There were no bathroom facilities and one water outlet for many families. When someone had to go to the bathroom, they would drop it on a piece of newspaper and then walk to the river and toss it in. Needless to say, the Pasig River was very polluted but the kids had nowhere else to swim. We established a route through the congested and tiny walkways of Pineda and began to give out a cup of warm breakfast for each child.

We wanted to build relationships and gain the trust of the adults and children. I fell in love with these beautiful people that had so little of the world's material goods, but seemed to be so happy and so content. My heart went out to each and everyone as the residents of Pineda were rapidly capturing my heart.

I teamed up with a couple of Filipino YWAM staff and we started an afternoon kids club two days a week on the basketball court along the river in Pineda. What we did was drive a vehicle down and park on the court; we would then put a karaoke machine on the hood of the vehicle, play music and teach the kids dance steps. Sometimes, we would have 30 or 40 kids out on the court doing steps to "This Little Light of Mine." I had so much fun! Here was this crazy American dancing around on the basketball court next to the Pasig River! I loved the kids and the kids loved me. I found myself literally wrestling on the ground with many of the boys in the concrete and dirt. Most of these children had skin diseases and were dirty, but it did not matter, I was experiencing God's heart for this neighborhood.

Stay Longer?

My outreach to the Philippines was scheduled for only two months, and then the plan was to fly back home, get a job and pay my parents back the money I borrowed for the airfare to get there. We had regular times of prayer and meetings with the base staff a couple times a week. Pretty much from the beginning of our outreach, the staff began to gently challenge us to pray and consider the possibility that God might want us to stay longer than just a few months. "Open your hearts and pray about a two-year commitment," was a mantra that kept ringing in our ears. The staff never gave up but kept gently challenging us just about every time we got together for prayer or a meeting.

This request was kept before me. At first, I thought that the request to stay longer was ridiculous (and honestly, it frightened me) because I had no money and was actually in debt. Besides, this was on the other side of the world and I needed to get back home and show off my "I've been overseas for Jesus badge," look down on and challenge everyone as to what they were doing for God. Because you see, I had finally arrived and now I was this important person that had obeyed God, gone around the world and now I needed to get back for everyone to see and admire! Oh man, was I in for a lesson!

About the 5th week, of our planned 8 week stay, I was walking up to the other house by myself (I thought I was by myself anyway) to get lunch. It seemed that the gentle request to just "pray about" a longer stay would not go away. I would wake up in the morning and God was there waiting for me with that request. As I was walking that day up to lunch, I was hearing the voice of God louder and louder. You know, because He loves us, if we are trying to ignore His whisper, sometimes He begins to shout! That was the case that day.

As I walked along, I could not shake His presence! I was hearing Him say, "What are you afraid of, just open up your heart and pray about it." I was really wrestling with God on this issue and trying to act like staying longer just did not make common sense (and it didn't) so God couldn't want me to do that. Almost to the other house, God turned it up and I could not ignore Him any longer. Out of frustration and irritation my attitude being in the category of "horrible", I finally stopped in the middle of the street, looked up, threw my hands in the air and practically shouted these words,

"Alright, alright! If that's what you want me to do, I'll do it."

Probably one of the sincerest prayers I have ever prayed and one that God said, "Hmm, not the best attitude, but it will do" because immediately, even instantly after saying that, the presence of God descended (I mean I felt the presence of God) on me in that street with His answer. Great amounts of peace and joy flooded my soul from above and I knew I was hearing from God. Instantly, I knew that I knew that I knew it was God's will for me to make a two-year commitment and to stay longer. In the matter of a few seconds, I went from fear and total frustration to new strength, joy, direction change and such excitement that I could barely contain myself.

I had heard from God and it didn't matter if He was asking me to make even a ten-year commitment, my heart was instantly converted to a long term missionary. Now, my head on the other hand was screaming at me with, "Are you nuts? You can't stay here longer. How are you going to live? Ron…… hello…… you have no money." God knew my head and that the enemy would try and talk me out of this, that's why I didn't walk anywhere for about a week, I floated. His presence was so strong, reassuring me that I was making the right decision and it was time for me to step up and be a big boy and learn to trust Him again, for everything.

I think I could write a book about learning to trust Him and how to grow in your relationship with Him. You can only trust someone to the degree that you know them and their character personally. I was being pushed again out of the "nest" of my comfort zone. It was time to learn how to "fly" on the downfall.

What this was revealing and uncovering in me, was the deception that I thought I had arrived and that I knew Him well enough to actually entrust Him with my life again. It was time to get out of the boat and supernaturally walk on the water! It was time to step into another level of relationship and trust.

So, I made the two-year commitment to stay and transferred from "student on outreach" to "full-time staff!" I wrote a few letters and mailed them back to New Song and a few other folks that I thought would consider financing my decision.

International phone calls were too expensive so letter writing was really the only economical way to communicate back home. Interesting thing was that a letter took about 8 days to go one-way and email was not around yet (I know it is hard to imagine life now without instant communications from just about anywhere on the planet). I mentioned earlier that New Song was one of the first churches to start to help. Being single, I really only needed about $250 to $300 a month to live very comfortably on the YWAM base and the financial support began to trickle in. God was faithful and people responded positively.

Still Running

I have to mention that when I arrived in Manila and recovered from the "jet lag" I greatly looked forward to resuming my running schedule that I had taken to a new level back in Hawaii. I was looking forward to running farther and faster than ever before. Long distance running is kind of like a drug! Endorphins are released in your body somehow and the "high" that develops with long distance running becomes addictive. I waited about 3 days and then strapped on my Nike's. I thought I was going to be ok until about 5 or 6 days later when my lungs started to get congested and my chest started to hurt.

I had never tried to run in such smoggy conditions and I soon realized I had to stop for health reasons. The air was just too polluted for sustained deep breathing in the Manila air. Heartbroken, I had to stop; the air was just too dirty.

Something Different About "Merlie"

"Rommel" was one of the first local guys that we met when we first arrived in January, 1989. He would hang out with us at the house, playing his guitar and singing. Anyway, not knowing where else to go to church on Sundays those first few weeks upon arriving in Manila, some of us followed Rommel to the church that he attended. "Pasig Evangelical Alliance Church" or "PEACH" was a short walk from our base and boasted a congregation of about 40 people that attended. We met Rommel's brother, "Harry" and their Mom that attended there also.

Harry was the drummer for the congregation and caretaker of the 3-story commercial building where the church met on the bottom floor. Harry also lived in a small room in the back of the church building.

One of the Sunday school teachers there in the church was a girl named "Merlie." I found out later that Filipinos were fond of nicknames and that her legal name was "Juliet." I think the first time I saw her was when she was peeking around the corner at me from the Sunday school room. I think I actually met her the second or third Sunday I was there in Manila. There was something definitely different about her. She was certainly not shy, that's for sure! I felt myself attracted to her right away, but told myself that I did not come over there to start a relationship. So, I pushed the feelings away and tried to just focus on what God had for me to do. Besides, at this point, I was only planning on being there for a few months. Well, long story short, we were friends for about 3 years, dated for a year and then we were married in Manila. Two of our three children were born in the Philippines.

I would actually stay 8 years there in the Philippines before moving my family back to the States in 1997. I really don't know how I can share even a small percentage of all I did in those 8 years in the islands.

It was Gods will for me to be there. "His Presence" and the overwhelming desire to go to the Philippines back in chapter one of this book when I was in high school rang true. This was a life calling for me. Even though I have at this point been back in the States for almost 20 years, my heart has never left. We have made numerous trips back to Asia to visit family and to vacation. I finally went back in August of 2015 for my first official ministry trip, having made an itinerary with pastors. More on that later, I am still not done with telling you about the squatter area, Pineda.

How Can I Ever Leave?

The precious people of Pineda had captured my heart. I was experiencing God's compassion for this group of impoverished, dislocated people. I worked in this squatter area for about a year and a half and today I am still in contact with several of the people I had built relationships with. Along with the morning feeding program and the Tuesday/Thursday afternoon "dance club" on the basketball court, I found out about a program through the "Philippine Bible Society" and started the third leg of my ministry in Pineda. The Bible Society would supply, at no charge, individual study pamphlets on books of the Bible. Written in their local language, the pamphlets had study tips and spaces to answer questions. You basically read the questions, studied your Bible and then wrote the answer in the spaces provided.

I started walking through Pineda one day after being there for about 6 months asking people if they wanted to sign up for this free program. I had won the trust and confidence of young and old and I soon was in charge of about 55 people that had signed up. I would go to Pineda weekly, pick up the completed study books, give them the next one in line and would almost always come back home with someone new that wanted to sign up and get started as well.

The Presence

I often think about the souls that I will recognize in Heaven because of the Philippine Bible Society and my efforts and ministry in the squatter area called Pineda. I really thought I would never be able to leave Pineda, how could I? I was so ingrained in the community that I actually asked the leadership at the YWAM base if I could move down there to live. I wanted to take baths on the sidewalk (in gym shorts) with a bucket of water and a dipper like the other men. I thought I was becoming more like Jesus who left paradise to come to earth. I was willing to sacrifice living in a big home in a nice neighborhood so that I could identify with a less fortunate and needy people. YWAM would not approve my request to move and live off base. As I look back on that now, if they had approved for me live down in Pineda, I bet I would have been asking to move back to the big house within a few weeks.

After a year and a half of living in Manila and breathing the polluted air, my health became negatively affected. I began to suffer from allergies and constant sinus congestion. My sinuses would not clear. They would clog up and become infected. I could buy antibiotics over the counter there and after a while, I was taking them almost like candy to clear out the infections. I started to lose weight and I could tell this was not going in a healthy direction. Long story short, I had to move out of Manila to cleaner air or I was going to get really sick. I had to say goodbye to Pineda and my precious friends.

By this time, I had already established a route out of Manila that I had traveled a few times. I have to go back to the first few weeks of arriving in Manila in January 1989. The big house that we lived in was owned by a family whose son lived just up the street about 5 houses. "Frank" and I became friends when we discovered one day that we were both scuba divers. Frank began inviting me to a nearby island where his Father lived and owned a house on the side of an island mountain. The family also had a rock quarry on the island and a business exporting granite rock.

So, I had already begun to take the two hour drive out of Manila to the pier city of "Batangas". From there we would board a boat for the hour long trip to the island of "Mindoro." By the way, if I have not mentioned it yet, it needs to be said, the Philippines consist of over 7,100 islands and there are many incredibly beautiful places. I thought I was in paradise as I took trips with Frank out to the island. He had friends there with scuba equipment that I could use and we would go diving.

I soon met other families out on the island of Mindoro. One family owned a very nice beach resort with of course, a tennis court. Well you guessed it, the owners of the resort had a son that was on the Philippine National Windsurfing Team and was also a tennis player. During that first year and a half, I would escape the Manila congestion, traffic and smog 5 or 6 times and hide out at Frank's Dad's place. We would go diving (yes, I have swam with sharks) and I would play tennis with my new friend. What a life! Suffering for Jesus! The contrast between living in Manila and staying on the side of an island mountain was like night and day. Frank's Dad's house was so far up the mountain that they did not even have electricity and I will never forget the slow, bumpy 20 minute ride it took to get up there. Fresh air was amazing! It seemed that my appetite almost doubled every time I went there and I also slept like a baby at night. This was definitely different when compared to my experience of life in Manila, which was seemingly non-stop heat, traffic jams and pollution.

Move to Batangas

Needing to get out of Manila for health reasons and being familiar with the area, I headed back out to the city of Batangas where YWAM had an outreach base. When visiting ministry teams would come through, I would help host them at the base.

I was at the base in Batangas for about a year. I met several of the local pastors and started working with a student ministry. I eventually stepped out of YWAM while I lived in Batangas and moved in with "Pastor Jun," one of the local pastors. It was while I lived with Pastor Jun that the romance with Merlie started to develop past friendship. I remember having to go down to the telephone office in downtown Batangas, stand in line and wait for a long distance phone booth so I could call her at her work. Phones were not available yet for every home.

While I was there in Batangas, I also went to see a local ear, nose and throat doctor about an operation on my sinuses to see if I could get some relief from congestion which had led to the infections I had suffered from in Manila. We scheduled an operation and I went into the hospital in Batangas, which could be considered a third world facility. I trusted the doctor, who had trained medically in the US, but after I came through the operation and woke up in the recovery room, the attendants needed to take me to the third floor where I was to share a room overnight. The elevator was broken in the hospital so two guys had to carry me on a stretcher up three flights of stairs. Thank God they never dropped me! I shared a room overnight with some Filipinos that had gotten hurt when the construction frame they were working on collapsed.

Back to Manila

I moved back to Manila after being in Batangas for about a year and a half. My relationship was getting serious with Merlie and I had also learned about a Bible School that I wanted to attend called, "Calvary Bible Institute." This was a one-year practical theology school that was sponsored by a church at one of the busy intersections in Manila called, "Crossing." Crossing was close to Capitolio and the Pasig Evangelical Alliance Church where I had met my future wife.

While I was going to the school, I lived with Harry (the drummer and building caretaker) at PEACH. Harry had his little room in the back of the building that he called home but was not big enough for both of us, so I lived in the sanctuary and slept on the church pews while I was going to school. It was a short ride from "home" to Crossing and the school. I had already perfected the art of riding in the "jeepneys" that were privately owned and used for most of the public transportation, along with busses and trikes (motorcycles with sidecars) in Manila. The jeepneys were the most fun and adventurous!

Jeepneys are long passenger vehicles with an open rear end where passengers would step in and out of. On the back of the jeepneys were these big bumpers that if you were brave enough, you could stand on the bumpers and hold onto handrails that were on the roof of the jeepney. It was dangerous but so much fun! You could look up over the roof and see what was coming, with the wind in your hair! I remember having several conversations with American Mormon missionaries as we hung off the back of jeepneys tearing through Manila traffic.

Let's Pull the Trigger

Merlie and I had talked to her parents about getting married but her Mom was not completely accepting of me yet. Her Dad and I had a pretty good relationship even though we couldn't really communicate verbally because my Tagalog (the local language they spoke) was insufficient and he didn't really speak English. Merlie was a college graduate so, her English was good. I did not know her Mom spoke broken English until out of the frustration of her daughter possibly marrying a foreigner and taking her daughter even further away from the Catholic Faith, she spoke up one day.

You see, the Philippines has been for a long time a predominantly Roman Catholic nation until the Protestant or "Born Again" church started to grow. Merlie was raised a Roman Catholic. Before I met her and while she was going to Engineering School, Merlie was invited to a student led campus Bible Study. This is where she discovered that religious activity was not what God wanted; He wanted a personal relationship with her.

Out of respect for her mother and desiring to have her "blessing" on our marriage, we postponed our plans to wed. We thought this would be a good time for my future wife to get some YWAM training and give her Mom some more time to warm up to me.

Merlie was working for the Philippine government in social work as a family advocate. She quit her job and I helped support her as she signed up for a YWAM school there in Manila (the same kind of school I had done in Salem). This also consisted of a 3 month lecture phase and a 2 month evangelistic outreach to an island that required an overnight boat ride to get to. We thought that because we were planning a life together, we might as well use this time for her to get some of the same training that I had gone through.

Ron the Evangelist

I have to tell you about some of the crazy things I did in the Philippines as an evangelist. I felt led by the Holy Spirit to preach just about anywhere. Sometimes when I was on a public bus I would stand up and start preaching. I think I was kind of like a modern day "John the Baptist," crying out in the wilderness. I had memorized several Tagalog "preaching lines" and I had a 45 second sermon I loved to share. When I was previously living in Batangas, I enrolled in a Tagalog school and tried to get a handle on the local language. It was one of the toughest things I had ever tried to do.

Anyway, I was still going to the Bible school at "Crossing" when the day arrived that Merlie was scheduled to be back from her YWAM outreach from one of the distant islands called "Palawan". A Filipino friend and I decided to take the two hour public transportation trip across Metro Manila to pick her up at the pier when she would be getting off the boat. We were on a roll that day. We were preaching in the jeepneys and busses all the way to the pier. When we finally arrived at the pier, I thought I was done "crying out" for the day. God had other plans.

We had arrived a little bit early at the pier and the arrival time of the boat was still about an hour away. The longer we waited; more people began to gather until there was a good sized crowd. Well, just like when I was at the Mormon Church in Elgin, the Holy Spirit moved in and on me, and I knew I had to preach to this crowd. Yes, my evangelistic gift was about to be exercised again.

I climbed up on a metal barrier, grabbed a hold of the edge of the roof of the small security guard shack that protected the entrance to the pier and gave it my best, "Cry in the wilderness." About the third time through my 45 second sermon, a gentleman from the crowd could not take it anymore, but had to respond.

From looking at his clothes, I am pretty sure he was of the Muslim faith. No one seemed to be paying any attention to me until he came out of the crowd and started shouting back at me. He told me that, "I didn't have the truth and that I didn't really have any love in my heart."

I looked down at him from my metal barrier pulpit not sure what to do, so I just started my sermon over again. He walked away only to come back again shouting the same thing just a minute later. Well, suddenly I was getting lots of attention and an even larger crowd was forming. I could see people actually running over to where we were because of the commotion going on between this man and myself. I believe it was his third time to come out of the crowd to speak to me when he said, "If you have love in your heart, then come down here and give me a kiss on the cheek." It was a challenge and one that probably at least a hundred and fifty Filipinos eagerly watched to see what I was going to do. This was another reason I believed he was of the Muslim faith because that is common to their religious practices.

Talk about on the spot! He stood there looking up at me and waited for my response. The crowd went silent as they waited for this drama to unfold. I felt God's compassion and love for this man so, in front of the watching crowd and thinking to myself, "What do I have to lose?" I jumped off the barrier, walked over to him and kissed him on the cheek. What happened next took me by surprise. The man, with nothing more to say, out of frustration just had to turn and walk away. The crowd erupted in loud cheers. Yes, cheers just like I had won the Super Bowl or something (sorry, just watched #50 yesterday). I was immediately surrounded by the crowd that wanted to shake my hand and congratulate me. I felt like a rock star! My friend and I that I was with, handed out all the gospel tracks we had in our possession and tried to talk to those that wanted to hear more about this message I had shared.

Are You Warm yet Mom

Merlie was back from her outreach so we started making plans again to get married. I think her Mom must have felt like we had honored her wishes and at least waited. She was ready this time to give us her blessing. We were glad we waited.

We were married January 23rd, 1993. I was already 33 years old, Merlie 7 years younger. We had a church wedding right there in Capitolio, Pasig Metro Manila. We honeymooned out to the island of Mindoro, staying in a little bamboo hut on one of the beaches. When we got back to Manila after the honeymoon, Merlies' Mom wanted us to stay with them at their home, which was a common practice in the Philippines. Well, that lasted about a week and I knew we had to secure other arrangements. I was thankful for the offer, but we needed our own space.

Merlie and I were able to rent an apartment about a 10 minute ride from Capitolio and 15 minutes from "Crossing" and the school. That was important because I had graduated from the one year Bible school and was going to join the school staff as the "Student Outreach Coordinator" and Merlie had enrolled as a student. We were pregnant three months into the school and my wife was about ready to have our first child when she walked the aisle to graduate.

As "Student Outreach Coordinator" for the school, I was involved in leading student teams on evangelistic outreaches. One of my favorite teams was the "Film Evangelism Team." We would fill our school jeepney with students, (the jeepney held about 15 passengers and there was always room for one more in the Philippines!) an 8mm reel to reel projector, the Philippine movie called "Hinugot sa Dilim", (which means in English "Snatched from the Darkness") a generator and puppets. Then we would head out of town for three day crusades and ministry.

The Presence

One of the favorite places we discovered was a small fishing village in Batangas at a small beach community called, "Laiya." Laiya was about a four hour drive from Manila and consisted mostly of white sand, blue sea, fishing boats and little bamboo homes that the fisherman and their families lived in. I remember feeling strongly that I had found the place where I wanted to retire! Laiya was such a simple place with wonderfully simple people. I was tempted to just kick off my shoes, eat fish, rice and vegetables and walk the beach for the rest of my life. When we first went there, there wasn't even any electricity in the village. So at night, when darkness fell, we cranked up the generator, hung up a bed sheet and showed the film. Earlier we had performed dramas and puppet shows. The puppets seemed to draw the biggest crowds. I'll bet that on our first trip there, that there were at least 200 children and adults that gathered for our ministry. We worked with and alongside Pastor "Bernie" who was establishing a church in the village.

We would arrive on a Friday, stay through the church service Sunday morning and then pack up and drive (I was usually the driver) back to Manila. I think it was my second time to Laiya that we had an encounter with God that I will never forget.

Why are People Crying

On this particular Sunday in Laiya, one of the students was tagged to preach Sunday morning in Pastor Bernie's church. I was enjoying the enthusiasm of the student preacher (although I was not really able to follow what he was saying) when I began to notice behind me that some people were starting to cry. I thought it was odd but tried to focus on the sermon. A few minutes later the crying got louder and more people joined in. I turned around to look and try to see what was going on and then back to the student preacher when all of a sudden, he just stopped preaching.

The crying was getting louder and there was no way we could ignore it any longer. It was then that I realized we were in the middle of a supernatural outpouring of the presence of God.

While Peter was still speaking these words, the Holy Spirit fell upon all those who were listening to the message. Acts 10:44

This was a divine visitation from God and we were in the midst of a real revival. God's presence was very strong. We started to lay hands and pray for people as the Holy Spirit poured Himself out! Before long, we had people lying all over the floor, weeping and being touched deeply by the Spirit of God. I remember Pastor Bernie at a loss of what to do. We both had not experienced an outpouring like this before. This lasted about 25 or 30 minutes and then His Presence lifted. After the service that morning, we were done with our outreach and needed to get going back to Manila. We heard incredible reports of the fruit of our ministry that weekend and how God almost tripled the size of the youth group and doubled the size of the church because of the outpouring. We blew in, blew up and then left the Pastor to manage the results.

Twenty-one years later, Pastor Bernie is still there in Laiya. My 15 year old son, Jacob, and I were just there in August of 2015. I had the privilege of speaking in his church and meeting again some of the people that are still there. One young man who is probably about 33 today remembered me from the outreaches before. He was probably about 8 of 9 years old when I first went to Laiya.

One Key I learned In School

I have to share one of the key lessons and experiences I had when I was a student at Calvary Bible Institute and before I joined the staff and became the schools' student outreach coordinator.

Most of the instructors and staff of the school were foreigners (like myself), being from the USA and Canada, graduates of and influenced by RHEMA Bible Training School in Tulsa, Oklahoma and Christ for the Nations Institute in Dallas, Texas.

One of the Instructors taught a class on the power of our words and that words were spiritual containers and could be motivated by Heaven or Hell! An easy example to help understand this principle is how a married couple can build up and encourage one another in their marriage with words or tear it apart by fighting and arguing, ending in divorce, the death of a union.

Death and life are in the power of the tongue, And those who love it will eat its fruit. Proverbs 18:21

For we all stumble in many ways. If anyone does not stumble in what he says, he is a perfect man, able to bridle the whole body as well. Now if we put the bits into the horses' mouths so that they will obey us, we direct their entire body as well. Look at the ships also, though they are so great and are driven by strong winds, are still directed by a very small rudder wherever the inclination of the pilot desires. So also the tongue is a small part of the body, and yet it boasts of great things. See how great a forest is set aflame by such a small fire! James 3:2-5

This particular instructor started to teach us about words and the power of confessing God's Word over our lives (something I was very ignorant of). At first, I thought this man was dangerous and I did not want to sit very close because of possible lightning bolts right there in the classroom! I had never heard anything like it in my Christian walk prior to this.

I had never seen or experienced such boldness in the presence of God, but it would be something that would set me more free than ever before and would help me experience God in a much different and deeper way than I had before.

Many believers struggle with their new identity in Christ and this is one reason why God's Word talks so much about renewing our minds and establishing new thoughts that better line up with His Precious Word. We need to rethink how we identify ourselves now that we have been spiritually "Born Again" and are "New Creatures in Christ", ("Christ" is not Jesus' last name, "Christ" means the "Anointed King"). Hence, Jesus the Anointed King or Christ.

Therefore if anyone is in Christ, (the anointed King) *he is* **a new creature; the old things passed away; behold, new things have come. 2 Corinthians 5:17**

Someone that has been translated from darkness to light and that is now found in the anointed King had better start thinking different about many things. This subject is another book but I will try to abbreviate one of the most powerful experiences I have ever had.

In the classroom that day, this instructor was teaching us how to take God's Word, claim it for ourselves and apply it practically. The teacher gave us an example of how he prays right there in the classroom.

He started pacing and walking back and forth in front of the class praying, thanking, praising and confessing, "Father, I thank you that I am the righteousness of God in Christ Jesus" and then this, "Father, I thank you that you have removed my sin from me as far as the East is from the West."

"Whoa! Wait just one minute," I thought, those were two of the most dangerous statements I had ever heard. Here was this guy claiming and saying right there in front of us that he was the "Righteousness of God in Christ" and that God had "Removed his sin from him as far as the East is from the West."

"Everybody stand back! Lightning is about to split the ceiling in the room," is what was running through my mind. What was happening is that my un-renewed mind was being exposed. I had no idea how far I had to go in the renewing of my mind so that I could, "Prove the will of God".

Therefore I urge you, brethren, by the mercies of God, to present your bodies a living and holy sacrifice, acceptable to God, which is your spiritual service of worship. And do not be conformed to this world, but be transformed by the renewing of your mind, so that you may prove what the will of God is, that which is good and acceptable and perfect. Romans 12:1-2

But you did not learn Christ in this way, if indeed you have heard Him and have been taught in Him, just as truth is in Jesus, that, in reference to your former manner of life, you lay aside the old self, which is being corrupted in accordance with the lusts of deceit, and that you be renewed in the spirit of your mind, and put on the new self, which in *the likeness of* God has been created in righteousness and holiness of the truth. Ephesians 4:24

These verses tell of at least three things. The first is that the Apostle Paul was encouraging us to actually present our bodies, "Acceptable to God." Acceptable to God? What was that? Up until now in my relationship with God, I had struggled deeply, like so many other believers, with a subject that the enemy just loves.

That subject is "condemnation" and feeling like you're never good enough, you blew it again and now even God can't forgive you. Have you learned yet that often times the most difficult person to get forgiveness from is yourself? When we truly and sincerely repent from our sin (rebellious acts) and mistakes, God's forgiveness is instant. Now, the devil will rarely ever say, "I forgive you." No, he will constantly try to condemn you for your sin and mistakes, even after God has forgiven you. The enemy loves to tell us that, "you're not good enough for God to forgive you, you've sinned too many times and now even God can't forgive you" leaving you with no hope and no way out. The other tough cookie to get forgiveness from is You or Yourself! There is a reason why the Apostle Paul urged "You" to present "Your body" as a living and holy sacrifice, acceptable to God. I don't think you can do that unless you first receive God's forgiveness, and then you follow it up with forgiving yourself.

The second thing that stands out in these verses in order for me to "prove what the will of God is", is that I have to be transformed by the renewing of my mind. I have to have new thoughts and I can't prove and or fulfill God's plan and destiny without new thoughts, without hitting the "reset" button for my mind; a reset for success. "Wait a minute," I thought, "I'm pretty happy with the thoughts I have." God was ready and preparing to take me somewhere in my thinking where I had not been yet or had discovered.

The third is that I actually have to do something! I must lay aside the old self, I must put on the new self and I must be renewed in the spirit of my mind which in the likeness of God has been re-created!

As the class went on that week, the instructor kept showing up, teaching us the same principle, everyday. "Interesting," I thought,

"God hadn't killed him yet."

So, I started to think that maybe it's safe for me to venture "out of the boat" and try applying this for myself as well. I still remember when I started to pray the way this instructor had showed us in class, it was scary. I had never been "out of the boat" on this open sea and walking on these uncharted waters. I had to try it though; the life that was released in the classroom had drawn me and was leading me forward. At home, I would go to our upstairs bedroom and begin to walk back and forth across the room with my Bible in my hands confessing the Word of God over my life. I worked my way gently into it because I still wasn't too sure if it was ok to say these things or if it was safe to pray this way. Actually present my body as acceptable to Him and claim that, "I was the righteousness of God in Christ" (actually put voice to this opinion and act like the blood of Jesus was enough?) and thank Him that He had, "Removed my sin from me as far as the East was from the West" (by the way, that's a long ways!) I felt like I was definitely treading on thin ice, at best, and I wasn't really too sure that I would make it out of the room alive.

I have a question for you, dear reader; if you can't stand and take a stand on the Word of God, then what are you standing on? You're probably standing on your experiences and your feelings like I had been doing up to that point.

For if by the transgression of the one, death reigned through the one, much more those who receive the abundance of grace and of the gift of righteousness will reign in life through the One, Jesus Christ. Romans 5:17

Therefore if anyone is in Christ, he is a new creature; the old things passed away; behold, new things have come. 2 Corinthians 5:17

He made Him who knew no sin to be sin on our behalf, so that we might become the righteousness of God in Him. 2 Corinthians 5:21

As far as the east is from the west, So far has He removed our transgressions from us. Psalms 103:12

After I began to pray this way in my "upper room" a few times and wasn't struck by lightning, a strange confidence and boldness began to rise up on the inside of me. Instead of tiptoeing across the room and whispering, I stepped completely "out of the boat," onto the raging sea and began to aggressively proclaim and confess His Word over my life. When Peter stepped out of the boat, there was something that he had to overcome before he could begin to walk on the water. That something was "fear". I began to experience a new freedom and level of fearlessness and energy that I had not experienced before in the presence of God. His Word is truth and it is powerful and God was beginning to lead me somewhere in my thinking that I had never been before. Remember what is in the power of the tongue? Death and life!

There are ceilings and barriers out there that need to be broken. One of those barriers is the barrier of limited thinking.

A "Barrier" is defined as:

A fence or other obstacle that prevents movement or access, a circumstance or obstacle that keeps people or things apart or prevents communication and progress.

The Neighbor, "Willie"

I will never forget one of the next door neighbors at the apartment complex where my wife and I and our small infant son "Robbie" first lived. His name was 'Willie" and he worked at a local bank somewhere in Manila. Willie also loved a certain musical artist named Michael Jackson! I had the opportunity to visit him in his upstairs room one day, only to see at least three or four posters of Mr. Jackson on the wall. He also loved to play Michael's music at a high volume.

Willie would sometimes crank up his music while I was trying to pray! At first it annoyed me and I wanted to go over and ask him to please turn it down. After this happened a few times, I had had enough. I did not go over and ask him to turn it down, I simply told myself that if he was comfortable enough to "invade my air space" with his music and not be concerned about his neighbor being disturbed, then I was going to return the favor and not be concerned about "invading his air space" with turning up the volume of praying and confessing.

If he wasn't embarrassed about filling the air with Mr Jackson, then neither would I be embarrassed about filling the air with my prayer and the Word of God. I know as I turned up the volume of "Thanking and Praising" and confessing the Word, Willie had to have heard me next door, as well as most of the neighborhood too.

I had started out on this spiritual journey and was headed somewhere where I had never been before! I felt like a modern day Moses that God was calling to hike up on a mountain and into His fiery presence. I suddenly would not be deterred by the fear of man or the enemy's condemnation anymore (or by what the neighbors thought) and I began to throw myself at the feet and mercies of the Word of God! It was shamelessly and fearlessly come into His Presence or die trying!

Something Popped!

I think I was about two weeks into praying like this when I had a very powerful experience with God the Holy Spirit. I was declaring who I was in Him very boldly (didn't really care who was listening because I felt like I was in a battle for my very life) and I was beginning to feel like I was taking serious ground from the enemy with my aggressive "thanking" and "praising" and confessing of the Word. This is what happens when you do that! You.......

Enter His gates with thanksgiving And His courts with praise. Give thanks to Him, bless His name. Psalms 100:4

You enter His gates, His courts and His freedom with thanksgiving and praise and that morning as I turned the corner in my "upper room" (a literal 180) and started out back across the room aggressively praying and proclaiming, something mind altering happened. Almost like a gun, something went off in my head; I felt something "snap." It is difficult to explain with words because it was more of a spiritual sensation than a physical one. Towards the front of my brain I experienced a loud "pop," as if something had just been aggressively broken. I immediately sensed an incredible release and freedom in my thinking. It was dramatic and powerful. It felt like I had walked out of a smoky, foggy room in my thinking and stepped into a room where I could see for a mile with a mind that had suddenly been set free.

For the word of God is living and active (alive and powerful, full of energy) and sharper than any two-edged sword, and piercing as far as the division of soul and spirit, of both joints and marrow, and able to judge the thoughts and intentions of the heart. (Amplified) Hebrews 4:12

The Word of God that I was confessing over my life and taking personally for myself had the ability to "pierce" and "judge" the thoughts and intentions of my heart. I was experiencing the transforming of my life by the "renewing of my mind" talked about in Rom 12:1-2. Wow! Fresh new freedom in my thoughts! The Word of God is living, active, alive and powerful, full of energy and when the Word dwells in abundance in your heart and you are bold enough to confess it with your mouth over your life, breakthroughs happen and the mind begins the renewing process. I was learning that "strongholds" are thought patterns, or ways of thinking, that you are ignorant or unaware of that effectively hold you back, hold you down and keep you from becoming all that God has destined you to be in Christ. Again a "Barrier" is a fence or other obstacle that prevents movement or access, a circumstance or obstacle that keeps people or things apart or prevents communication and progress.

Strongholds and Fortresses

These things called "strongholds" are set up and established in our minds and most of the time we don't even know they exist. It just seems normal, but they are incompatible thought patterns that do not agree with our new Identity and the "new creature in Christ" that we have become.

For though we walk in the flesh, we do not war according to the flesh, for the weapons of our warfare are not of the flesh, but divinely powerful for the destruction of fortresses (or the pulling down of strongholds NKJV). We are destroying speculations and every lofty thing raised up against the knowledge of God, and we are taking every thought captive to the obedience of Christ, 2 Corinthians 10:-5

The above verse says that we are taking every what captive? Yes, every thought captive! I used to think that "pulling down strongholds" would only happen when I could go up on a mountain and pray against the enemy in the air. I would not completely discount or count that out, but now I would definitely put more credit defining "strongholds" as thought patterns in our minds. These patterns are something that the enemy can hide behind and influence us in our thinking.

Judgment happened that day. God's Word and His Spirit reached deep into my mind and thoughts, then they pulled the not so "merry-go-round" or "pattern" of thoughts that were designed to keep me down, and not allow me to rise to my new position in Christ, lined them up against a firing squad wall and said, "This destructive and suppressive mental activity will no longer will be allowed to dwell here! Bam! Get out!" Their hideous dark power to control and influence was dissolved and broken.

"Strongholds are designed by the enemy, our carnal nature and our un-renewed mind to hold you down and suppress you"

The enemy did not like what happened in my upper room that day. Ignorance, false guilt, condemnation and shame began to lose its death grip over my mind and subconscious thinking. The scripture in the Bible is clear, at the end of Heb 4:12 it says, "The Word (anointed by the Spirit) has the ability to judge or arrest the thoughts and intentions of the heart." The Word of God, the Spirit of God and my obedience and boldness had begun to accomplish the revealing and emerging of a new identity in Christ (the anointed King).

What is Vision?

Vision is an internalized, clear mental picture of a preferable future and a result of God imparting to your spirit man. Vision is seeing your end from the beginning. When you look out at your future, what do you see? If all you can see is darkness and no hope, then get ready for God to replace that with a mental image of a preferable future. God gives us the gift of being able to go into our future, look at it, study it, taste it, and then come back and say,

"I want to go there"!

Sight is a function of the eyes; vision is a function of the heart. You were not born, nor created, to live by your eyes. Your eyes show you what is; vision shows you what could be. Vision is a glimpse of your purpose. Vision is seeing your purpose in Technicolor. What has God shown you from an early age? What have you seen yourself clearly doing in the future? In the book of Genesis, God showed a teenager named Joseph his future in dreams. God showed him a futuristic vision of him sitting on a throne and his older brothers bowing down to him. When he shared that with his family, it got him in a lot of hot water and trouble, but as he stayed faithful to God through all the tests and trials, the vision and dream came to pass. God had given him a vision and showed him his future in a dream.

The Vision of October 13th, 1993

I have to share a vision that God gave me on the morning of October 13th, 1993 in Manila. This came shortly after I experienced the dramatic "pulling down of strongholds" I just wrote about.

That morning, I was awake early reading, praying, confessing and meditating on God's Word. God spoke to me very clearly with a vision, so clearly that I wrote down the date and the experience in my Dr Ryrie New American Standard Study Bible. I documented it. That is a very important point I want to make right now. When God speaks to you about your future in dreams and visions, write it down immediately. This is the events that took place that morning.

I was first reading Paul's prayer for the saints in Ephesus in Eph 1:15-18.

For this reason I too, having heard of the faith in the Lord Jesus which exists among you and your love for all the saints, do not cease giving thanks for you, while making mention of you in my prayers; that the God of our Lord Jesus Christ, the Father of glory, may give to you a spirit of wisdom and of revelation in the knowledge of Him. I pray that the eyes of your heart may be enlightened, so that you will know what is the hope of His calling, what are the riches of the glory of His inheritance in the saints Ephesians 1:15-18

I pray that the eyes of your heart may be enlightened? What in the world are the eyes of your heart? I like to call it your dream and vision center. Your dream and vision center is where God can show you past, current and futuristic events. The "eyes of my heart" were enlightened that morning and the "spirit of wisdom and of revelation" was moving as I continued reading and meditating on Galatians 5:22,

But the fruit of the Spirit is love, joy, peace, patience, kindness, goodness, faithfulness, gentleness, self-control; against such things there is no law. Galatians 5:22-23

And then I went on to spend time in John 7:37-38.

Now on the last day, the great day of the feast, Jesus stood and cried out, saying, "If anyone is thirsty, let him come to Me and drink. He who believes in Me, as the Scripture said, 'From his innermost being will flow rivers of living water. John 7:37-38

I was confessing God's Word that morning, declaring that the fruit of His Spirit was growing in my spirit and that from my innermost being, rivers of living water was flowing from my innermost being. As I pressed into God and into His presence that morning the eyes of my heart became enlightened and God showed me an amazing vision. What I saw were nations (or people groups) coming to eat of His Fruit that was growing in my spirit, nations (or people groups) coming to drink of His Rivers of Living Water (the presence and movement of the Holy Spirit) that was flowing from my innermost being. I saw it and I documented it, in other words, I wrote down the date and what God showed me in my Bible.

This speaks of two things to me now. First, that God has called me to impact Nations. Second, that right now, around the world, nations are coming to eat of His Fruit that is growing in our spirits, the corporate Body of Christ, and that nations are coming to drink of His rivers of Living Water that is flowing through our corporate innermost beings.

This was not only a vision of my future but a vision of and what is happening right now in and through the corporate Body of Christ (the anointed King) on the planet.

It will come about after this That I will pour out My Spirit on all mankind; And your sons and daughters will prophesy, Your old men will dream dreams, Your young men will see visions. Joel 2:28

I continue to see this vision with the eyes of my heart. It is something that I continue to hold onto as I try and stay on course with the plan God has for me. This principle is true: If you can see your destination, it controls your decision making. God is a God that wants to show us our end from the beginning. Your future is not ahead of you, it is inside of you. Your future is God's history.

I have had several more dreams and visions in the last 12 months that I am not at liberty to share with you now. I will have to include them in future writings as God gives me liberty.

Weapons against the Spirit of Depression

While I was in the Philippines for a total of eight years, I was able to fly back and forth to the USA to visit family and supporters just about every other year. I remember being there once without going home for a full two year period and that was a long time without seeing my American family or standing on American soil. In June, of 1994, I took my little family of my wife and first born infant son, "Robbie," home to the States for an almost three month stay. We split our time in the States staying with my family in Elgin and going back and forth to Portland and other places to visit friends and supporters. This was a long time to be away from Manila and the adjustment back to the culture of the Philippines and Manila life was dramatic and very difficult for me when we returned.

It was back to the seemingly unending heat, traffic, smog, congestion, sweating and garbage piled up on just about every street corner. It was overwhelming and more than I wanted to have to adjust back to. I began asking myself, "Why did I come back here?" I had adjusted to the fresh, clean cool air, green grass, no humidity and clean cities back in Oregon. This really bothered me for the first few weeks after my return to Manila.

The more I complained about the conditions in Manila and questioned whether I should have come back or not, the more discouraged I became. I realized that I was heading in a downward spiral to the land called "Depression." I had never experienced these debilitating feelings as deep as I was at that time. I could tell that if something did not change pretty quickly, I was going to be in real trouble.

I sought the Lord and cried out for help. God spoke to me very clearly. He said something very simple to me, He said "Give Thanks." That's it. He told me to start giving thanks. Well, that was something I really did not feel like doing but I knew I had to do something different. I unwillingly started to thank Him and praise Him. Somehow I knew my life depended on it.

I started to thank and praise Him for bringing me back to Manila, for the heat, the smog, the traffic, the grey dirty buildings and the garbage on every corner. I struggled at first and it was really difficult. "Thank you for bringing me back Lord! Thank you, thank you, thank you!" "Praise You for bringing me back Lord, praise you, praise you, praise you." God's Word again is clear:

Enter His gates with thanksgiving And His courts with praise. Give thanks to Him, bless His name. Psalms 100:4

You will make known to me the path of life; In Your presence is fullness of joy; In Your right hand there are pleasures forever. Psalms 16:11

It took a very concentrated, focused effort on my part and It was actually a lot of work. I could tell that I was going against everything my physical body and senses did not want to do. It took hours of prayer and several days before I noticed any results.

After about 2 days of almost non-stop thanking and praising, the fog of depression began to lift off of my life. I know now that I was in a spiritual battle with the dark forces of depression. The enemy has no answer for a saint that will draw near to God in praise and thanksgiving.

I can't say that I am this incredibly disciplined person, but I know that the "lazy, unwilling to open their mouths and get down on their knees and fight believer" would not have had the same dramatic results that I experienced. The joy returned! The strength returned and suddenly I was pumping my fist in the air, once again knowing that God had called me to the Philippines and that I was in the center of God's will for my life. I was ready for a so called, "second round" of life and ministry in the Philippines and I was ready once again, with fresh strength and joy, to face the trials and differences of this foreign country on the other side of the planet.

Some might consider this cruel and insensitive, but I really believe that most "Believers" that are on prescription antidepressants (and I know a few personally, as you do) would greatly benefit from two or three days of concentrated Thank You, Thank You, Thank You's! Turn off the TV, cell phone and the internet for a few days and weeks, get on your knees and I believe that the results would be astounding. Results will come when we learn how to stand on His Word, open our mouths and fight! Death and life are in the power of......... Let's not be like Thomas, make a choice to rejoice now, before you see the Lord with your physical eyes. In His Presence is fullness of Joy!

The Protection of "Submission to Authority"

There was another lesson that I desperately needed to learn and I hope you're a quicker study than I was on this one. This next lesson only took me about 10 years to finally start to understand.

The vivid memory of being in Pastor Richard's office in the fall of 1988 and the fact that white, wild horses would not have been able to hold me back from heading out from my home church in Portland to the Philippines again comes crashing back right now. "Submission to Authority" or "Being Undercover" is a safety device that God has worked into His Kingdom and the Body of Christ that is for our protection and individual benefit. It is kind of like seeking your Father's advice before launching out in a new direction and being able to receive instruction, guidance and wisdom from those that have lived a little longer on the planet; a very good idea actually.

When I headed to Hawaii and then to the Philippines in January 1989, I did not have a clue what this safety net was all about. I really did not want to hear or listen to any counsel or advice, I was an emotional bull in a china shop and I just had to go. It was on the foreign mission field that God would begin to prepare me to learn the lesson, protection and blessing of this principle.

New Song Leaders and the Missions Board

As I mentioned earlier, when God spoke to me and I knew that God wanted me to stay longer than my two month outreach, New Song Church stepped up to the plate from the beginning to provide financial support. Because they were the largest donor in helping pay the bills, they wanted and expected me, to check in with them once in awhile and give them a report. I stayed in monthly contact by writing and mailing letters (snail mail letters was all the communications I had at the time) to New Song and other churches and a few individuals that were helping financially. I did not have a problem with the accountability and reporting that they were asking for and expecting. Their desires seemed reasonable and it only made good sense.

A pattern began to develop over the 8 years I was there. About every one and a half to two years I would move to a different city and begin working with a different ministry. About the 2nd or 3rd time I wrote to New Song about an exciting change and a "new" direction that I believed God was taking me in, they wrote back and told me that it would be good that before the next time I felt like God was taking me to a different location to work with a different ministry, that I should check in with them before I made the jump. The mission's board just wanted to know ahead of time so they could pray about it and help us in seeking God's direction. Of course I wrote back and said, "No problem, I can do that." Have you ever had something go in one ear and then right out the other? Well, I forgot to check in with them the next time I changed location and ministries about a year and a half later.

They warned me again and reminded me that they expected advance notice before I made any major changes in location or ministry. I said I was sorry and that I would surely let them know next time in advance if I felt like God was leading me in a new direction. In one ear and out the other! I still was not "getting it" and a year or so later did it again, contacting them only after the fact I had moved location and ministry.

The church leadership at that point decided to give me two options. New Song was done supporting me financially and rightfully so. The first one was that they were offering me one-way airfare for my family and I to fly home. The second option was to allow me to stay there without their continued financial support.

What was amazing about all of this at the time was that the power and grace that was on my life to be able to be away from my American family and friends, and not be overly "homesick", suddenly lifted and I thought I was going to die if I did not go home. God made it obvious to me that we were to take option one and take the money to pay for our airfare home. The Spirit of God made it ever so clear that it was time for me to take my wife, 2 year old son and 7 month old baby girl back to America.

Back to the States In 1997

The leaders at New Song wanted us to spend some time "debriefing" with them when we first came back. We stayed in Portland for a few weeks at the home of one of the elders from the missions board. After that, they released us to go live anywhere we wanted. The only desire and directive they gave was for me to "get a job" and not go back into full-time ministry.

So, soon after meeting with the leadership in Portland for a few weeks, we moved back to Elgin, my home town. We immediately plugged into a church in La Grande (19 miles from Elgin) who hired me as their part-time youth minister. I also started a ministry in Elgin which consisted of a Tuesday afternoon "Kids Club" and Thursday night church service. In one ear and out the other, I basically went into full-time ministry and did not look for a job.

God did some amazing things with our ministry in Elgin, but two things were happening. One, I was getting ahead of God and preparing to "go around the mountain again." Two, I had disregarded New Song's wisdom, advice and directive and still had not learned the protection and blessing of submission to authority!

Long story short, we lived this way for about a year and a half and then the wheels came off again. I was reduced to no ministry and having to look for a job to support my family. Shortly after this, someone from our church handed me a cassette tape by a man named "John Bevere", teaching on the subject of submission to authority from his book, "Under Cover." The lights came on. God spoke to me very clearly and showed me what had been happening in this area for the last 10 years. I still have a copy of the letter I wrote to Pastor Richard and the New Song Church Missions Board apologizing for my actions.

This Place is Falling Apart!

After returning from the Philippines, we were at this first church in La Grande for almost seven years, when something very strange began happening. The place just started to fall apart. It seemed like the protection we had previously had there was gone. People were leaving, one husband just walked away from his wife for no good reason and I suddenly felt exposed and unprotected.

I looked at my wife and three young children and thought to myself, "We have got to get out of here before something bad happens to us." So, we started visiting around to other churches in search of where God may be desiring to lead us. Nothing clicked, no bells, no whistles, but I knew we had to get to higher ground. God is faithful and showed up in a big, miraculous way. Enter the amazing provision, protection, guidance and direction of God!

Remember I told you earlier about Duane and the street evangelism team at New Song Church in Portland? Well, come to find out, Duane was friends with a man named Tom McReynolds when they were both high school students in Portland. Tom was currently living in La Grande and was the head Pastor of a church. Tom also owned a cabinet making business as well. Both the business and his church became too much to do, so Tom decided to resign from his church to devote himself full-time to his business.

That is when he called Duane. Duane moved his family from Portland to La Grande (260 miles) and took over the church and changed the name to "New Song." God literally wrote it in the sky for me to see! How could I not catch on that maybe God was leading us to New Song in La Grande? We have been a part of the church in La Grande now for almost 14 years. Now that's pretty amazing guidance, if I don't say so myself. Small world huh, but I would sure hate to have to paint it! Thank God for His never-ending, supernatural, miraculous guidance and protection.

Wrapping it Up!

Since coming back to the US in 1997, we have visited the Philippines and my wife's family that still remains there about once every year or two. Not all of us have gone back together to visit all the time. Sometimes it was just Merlie and I, sometimes a combination of just her and one of the children.

At the time of this writing, her Mom, Dad and older sister have already passed. She still has three brothers and their families to visit when we want too, although one of the three brothers now lives in Canada with his family.

In twenty years back in the States, I have had at least a half-dozen jobs and have currently sold real estate and refereed high school basketball and soccer for the last 6 years. I have really enjoyed the freedom of schedule that real estate has afforded me, especially when it came to watching my children play sports. My two oldest ran track and played soccer in high school.

They also both played soccer in college as well and I have probably been to most of their games and track meets. Our youngest son, Jacob (who is already taller than all of us), ran cross country and played tennis his freshman year in high school.

Three years ago, I signed up and became a Gideon. The Gideons are a group of volunteers that actively raise finances for the printing and distribution of Bibles. This organization is probably best known for being responsible for placing Bibles in motels. The young man that handed me that New Testament on the Mt Hood Community College campus years ago (I wrote about this experience in the first part of this book), was a volunteer with the Gideons. So, for years I have wanted to give back to the Gideons and be a volunteer bringing hope to more people like me who desperately needed contact with their Creator!

I have been privileged to speak in most of the churches in our local area as a Gideon, telling my story and raising finances to print more Bibles. As a Gideon, we are usually allowed 10 or 15 minutes to do a Gideons presentation and then at the end of the service stand at the back of the church with an open Bible, which allows people to come up and place their offering and support.

As I have begun my second and third season as a Gideon, more churches have allowed me to come and take the whole service time, not just 10 or 15 minutes. I have even been given the freedom and permission from the Gideons to stray from the traditional "Gideon Presentation" and just preach whatever God has put on my heart. This has been excellent training for what I believe God has for me in the future!

Where Is The Wealthiest Place On The Planet?

That is a question that rocked my world in the month of June, 2015. My wife and 19 year old daughter were in the Philippines for two weeks visiting family and vacationing. I was home in La Grande with our youngest son. My wife had ordered a book that arrived while they were overseas, "Releasing Your Potential" by Dr Myles Munroe. I started reading and realized that I had read some of his material years ago, had listened to some of his sermons and I remembered the life and the power of God that was on his material.

Anyway, I was really enjoying Dr Munroe's book when he penned the question, "Where is the wealthiest place on the planet?" Is it the diamond mines of Africa, the oilfields of Iraq or Iran or is the wealthiest place on the planet downtown Manhattan in New York? I thought it was a strange question to begin with and I soon realized that I was in the midst of a setup! His answer shook me to my core! His answer to the question was, "The graveyard!" The graveyard is the wealthiest place on the planet. The graveyard? What in the world was he trying to say? Dr Munroe went on to explain eloquently.

Consider this; God does not make anything without first giving it a purpose. You and I were given a purpose, an assignment at birth. Many, many people sadly, will never discover what that purpose and assignment is. So, on the inside of each and every one of us are gifts and callings. How many of us actually discover, in the course of life, what those gifts and abilities are and how many of us actually stir those gifts and abilities up, putting them into the use that God had intended? This is very sad to say, but not all of us. So, many, many of us just leave them there on the inside, undiscovered, unused and present with us when we die.

We take them to the grave and enrich the grave instead of pouring them out and being a blessing to humanity in the short time of life that God has given us on this planet. So, in the graveyard are books and poetry that were never written, businesses and ministries that were never started, movies that were never made etc, etc.

When I read that and God spoke to me, I felt like He hit me upside the head with a soft board. It pierced my heart and deeply convicted me. Sometimes, He has had to graciously do that to get my attention. I realized that God was speaking to me powerfully and what I had just read and understood was defining me and my current situation perfectly.

OMG That Is Me!

So I said something like this, "OMG that is me!" I knew that God had gifted me and had given me talents, that there was a calling, an assignment on my life that I needed to fulfill. I also realized that I was not currently and actively pursuing those things. I knew that God had called me to go around the world and preach the Gospel of the Kingdom (the Philippines being central in that assignment) and that I had placed that call on the back burner for some time now in my life.

I looked pretty good on the outside, going to church, speaking in churches as a Gideon, tithing and giving, but I knew on the inside I was void of life because my gifts laid dormant, unstirred and put away somewhere on a shelf. I was preparing to die very improperly. The Apostle Paul gives us an example of the correct way to properly leave earth.

For I am already being poured out as a drink offering, and the time of my departure has come. I have fought the good fight, I have finished the course, I have kept the faith 2 Timothy 4:6-7

Paul poured himself and his gifts out in ministry to the people God had called him to. A good soccer or basketball coach instructs his players to "leave it all on the field!" Paul was ready to die and was determined to and convinced that he was leaving it all on the field. He did not want to enrich the grave at his passing.

Ministry Trip #1

That encounter with God in June of 2015 on a Sunday morning before church, pierced me deeply and I realized that I needed to repent. My definition of "Repent" is:

Change Your Thinking And Return To Your High Place Of Luxury

When we are thinking right, we realize the Bible says we are seated with Christ in Heavenly places, a place of luxury! I immediately got on my knees and I wept, I cried and I said I was sorry. I also started to make plans that very morning to get back to the Philippines for a reason that I had not done in the last twenty years. That reason was to preach the Gospel of The Kingdom that had changed my life. I started to contact old friends and church leaders in the Philippines and it did not take me long to have an itinerary of places and dates to travel and minister. My youngest son Jacob, age 14 at the time, went with me just a few months later in August that year. Provision for the trip was miraculous.

Where God guides, He provides
Where He leads, He meets needs
Where He directs, He connects

I put a short video of my testimony on my Facebook page and let people know what our plans were for the 18 days we were planning to be gone in August and that if anyone wanted to pray for and support our trip financially, that it would be very much appreciated. Along with two churches in our local area that allowed me to come and preach before we left and took offerings to help pay for the trip, I had a friend on Facebook contact me saying that he and his wife wanted to help financially as well. We had over $5,000 come in which paid for the entire trip.

On this first trip, I was honored to travel and speak in several churches and see God move in miraculous ways. We caught up with Pastor Bernie, in the fishing village of "Laiya", where God had broken out in revival twenty-two years ago when I led the student ministry team there. (If you want to read that again, go back to page 97 "Why Are People Crying.") Jacob and I took a domestic flight from Manila down to one of the southern Philippine islands and visited my American missionary friends, Mark and Patti Kinney that have been there for 8 years. When we arrived, they told me that they considered me the "grandfather" of their ministry because of our long term relationship and the fact that when Patti was in high school, she came to her very first Bible study that I was leading when I was a part of the volunteer staff with J.T. and the high school ministry at New Song in Portland.

Mark and Patti also set it up for me to speak in one of the local churches on the one Sunday that we were there on their island. It was very exciting and I felt incredibly honored to be the guest of Mark, Patti and their Pastor and the guest speaker that morning in a very "lively" and crowded church. Jacob and I had a great time on this first trip and we saw God move miraculously.

One Year Later, Ministry Trip #2

My son Jacob approached me in May of 2016 and asked me a question. He said, "When are we were going back to the Philippines again?" That question greatly motivated me to seek the Heart of God and plan another trip. We took off just a few months later for 23 days in July/August of 2016. We had the privilege of catching up with a missionary friend of mine from Canada who has been living there for 25 years, Pastor Mark Deslippe.

Pastor Mark lives with his Filipina wife "Malou" and three children and oversees multiple churches in different areas of the Philippines. Jacob and I spent the first 11 days with their family traveling and ministering in outdoor crusades and Sunday services. We spent the last week with a new contact (another Pastor Mark) that I had just met on Facebook through a mutual friend before we left. God opened some incredible doors for ministry on this trip and for the near future. I am praying and anticipating that it will not be another whole year before I am on Philippine soil again.

When we move in and have our gifts stirred up, that is when we feel most alive. That is when we are fulfilling our assignment and fulfilling the purpose for why we are here on this planet. Traveling, preaching, teaching, writing and evangelism are what "cranks my tractor!" It is my purpose. I know at this point that I am not a Pastor. I would find it difficult to preach to the same crowd every week. Not all are called and gifted to go around the world and preach.

Your gift and assignment could be serving in your local church, starting businesses, writing books, making money to be a big giver, raising Godly children, art, song writing or a myriad of other things. The questions you need to ask yourself are these, "What cranks my tractor? What starts my motor? What do I lie awake at night dreaming of doing? Please don't stop daydreaming either; with God all things are possible.

Your Vision Gives You Energy
Your Purpose Gives You Fulfillment

I seem to be at the end of things here. I have so enjoyed God's presence and the quiet times in the middle of the night that the Holy Spirit and I have spent together writing this. I have found myself in tears many times as God has brought this all back vividly to my memory and I endeavored to type it into my computer so that it could be put into print and hopefully my first book that will touch, strengthen and encourage many. I hope this has left you wanting for more. Taste and see that the Lord is good!

Fulfilling the Vision

The vision that God gave me of "Nations coming to eat of His fruit and drink of His Spirit" back in October 1993 while I was in Manila has started to come to pass. With about two days left in our July/Aug 2016 ministry trip #2 to the Philippines, I received an email from a leader at the international headquarters of the Gideons ministry in Nashville, Tennessee. They invited me to come and share my testimony at their International "All In" Conference later that year in October. This Gideon conference consisted of national and international leaders in the Gideon ministry from all over the world. They flew me back to Tennessee from Oregon, all expenses paid, to speak for 10 minutes. Yeah, 10 minutes. They wanted to hear firsthand how my life had been impacted by one of their own handing me that Gideon Bible, 30 some years ago on that Community College campus. This opportunity humbled me.

I traveled with my 85 year old Dad "Spence" to Nashville and back. It was the first time in 40 years since he had been on an airplane. The Gideons put us up in the hotel for one night where the conference was being held.

I was so privileged to spend time with about 180 national and international leaders from around the world and to share my testimony before them. If you are interested in listening to my 10 minute story that they videotaped at the conference, you can go to my website provided below. I have it uploaded there where it is available to watch. **ronsmithauthor.com**

How many chapters are there in the Book of Acts? That's right, 28. Now let's you and I fulfill our purpose, stir up and exercise our gifts and get busy writing chapter 29. I hope we get to meet again soon.

You are gifted, you are called and you have a purpose. Thy Kingdom come, Thy will be done, on Earth as it is in Heaven. Your mistakes are not more powerful than your purpose and you will fulfill your purpose and assignment as you renew your mind and start to operate in the new identity that God has for you in Christ!

There is something very important that God wants to do on earth that makes your presence absolutely necessary!

I want to leave you with one more scripture, one of my favorites!

For I am **confident of this very thing, that He who began a good work in you will perfect it until the day of Christ (the anointed King) Jesus. Philippians 1:6**

Thank you for coming along with me on my short journey! I will be thinking about you and looking for you again soon, as I am already writing my next release. This is the end for now.

"Smitty"

ABOUT THE AUTHOR

Ron Smith grew up in the small logging community of Elgin, Oregon. He was a missionary in the Philippines for 8 years and graduated from "Calvary Bible Institute" in Manila. He is married with three children and currently lives in La Grande, Oregon with his Filipina wife named "Merlie". Ron is also a real estate agent, referees high school basketball and soccer and makes ministry trips to the Philippines.

To order bulk discounted copies of **"The Presence"** or to check out some of Ron's teaching videos like:

"The Kingdom of God"   or
"Vision, Seeing your End from the Beginning",

then please go to his website listed below.

ronsmithauthor.com

Follow Ron on his Personal and Business Facebook pages at:

https://www.facebook.com/ron.smith.589

https://www.facebook.com/RonSmithAuthor/

You can also email Ron at **"waysofroyalty@gmail.com"**

Made in the USA
San Bernardino, CA
12 March 2017